IRELAND'S BEST WALKS
A WALKING GUIDE

HELEN FAIRBAIRN is a full-time travel writer and has written numerous walking guidebooks, exploring destinations as diverse as America's Rocky Mountains, the European Alps and Scotland's highlands and islands. A regular contributor to *Walking World Ireland* magazine, Helen has spent years researching the best walking routes in Ireland. Her other walking guides for The Collins Press are *Dublin & Wicklow*, *Ireland's Wild Atlantic Way* and *Northern Ireland*.

The photographs in this book are the work of Irish landscape photographer **GARETH MCCORMACK**, author of *The Mountains of Ireland*. For more information or to license the images, see www.garethmccormack.com.

Looking towards Bunglas from the summit of Slieve League, County Donegal.

Disclaimer

Hillwalking and mountaineering are risk sports. The author and The Collins Press accept no responsibility for any injury, loss or inconvenience sustained by anyone using this guidebook.

Advice to Readers

Every effort is made by our authors to ensure the accuracy of our guidebooks. However, changes can occur after a book has been printed. If you notice discrepancies between this guidebook and the facts on the ground, please let us know, either by email to enquiries@collinspress.ie or by post to The Collins Press, West Link Park, Doughcloyne, Wilton, Cork, T12 N5EF, Ireland.

On the final approach to Benbaun, the highest point in County Galway. Twelve Bens, Connemara.

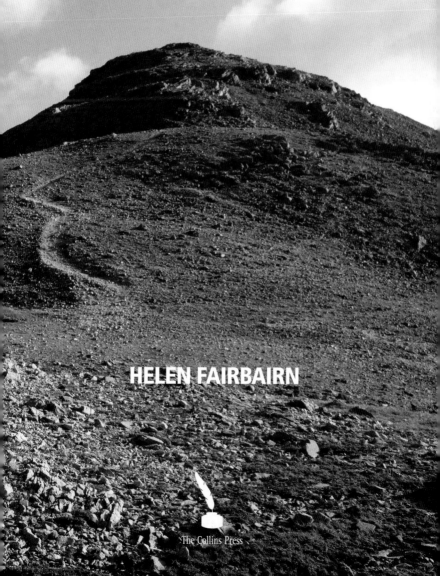

IRELAND'S BEST WALKS
A WALKING GUIDE

HELEN FAIRBAIRN

The Collins Press

First published in 2014 by
The Collins Press
West Link Park
Doughcloyne
Wilton
Cork
T12 N5EF
Ireland

Reprinted 2015, 2016, 2017

A CIP record for this book is available from the British Library.

Paperback ISBN: 978-1-84889-211-8
PDF ISBN: 9781848895331
ePub ISBN: 9781848895379
Mobi ISBN: 9781848895386

Design and typesetting by Fairways Design
Typeset in Myriad Pro
Printed in Poland by Białostockie Zakłady Graficzne SA

Evening light on the Cliffs of Moher, County Clare.

Contents

Southwest

Southeast

Looking over Coulagh Bay from the Coastguard Station Loop, County Cork.

Route Location Map

Northeast
1. Causeway Coast Path
2. Binevenagh Cliffs
3. The Antrim Hills
4. Sawel and Dart
5. Cuilcagh
6. Slieve Meelmore and Slieve Meelbeg
7. Slieve Donard
8. Slieve Muck
9. Slieve Bearnagh and the Silent Valley
10. The Binnians
11. Slieve Foye

Northwest
12. Melmore Head
13. Muckish
14. Errigal
15. Slieve Snaght and the Poisoned Glen
16. Glenveagh and Farscallop
17. Glencolmcille Circuit
18. Slieve League Traverse
19. Lavagh Beg and Lavagh More
20. Benbulbin and Benwiskin

West
21. Benwee Head
22. Achill Head and Croaghaun
23. Minaun Heights
24. Glendahurk Horseshoe
25. Nephin
26. Clare Island
27. Inishturk
28. Croagh Patrick
29. Mweelrea
30. Sheeffry Traverse
31. Ben Creggan and Ben Gorm
32. Diamond Hill
33. Glencorbet Horseshoe

34. Glencoaghan Horseshoe
35. Central Maumturks – North
36. Central Maumturks – South
37. Black Head
38. Cliffs of Moher Coastal Path

Southwest
39. Great Blasket Island
40. Brandon Mountain
41. Slieve Mish Circuit
42. Coomloughra Horseshoe
43. The Reeks Ridge
44. Coomasaharn
45. Gearhameen Horseshoe
46. Torc Mountain
47. Dursey Island
48. Cummeengeera Horseshoe
49. Hungry Hill
50. The Sheep's Head

Southeast
51. Galtymore
52. Lough Muskry Circuit
53. Knockmealdown Circuit
54. Nire Valley Coums
55. Coumshingaun

East
56. Howth Cliff Path
57. Great Sugar Loaf
58. Mullaghcleevaun
59. Luggala and Knocknacloghoge
60. Djouce and War Hill
61. Tonelagee
62. Scarr and Kanturk
63. Camaderry Circuit
64. The Spinc Loop
65. Lugnaquilla

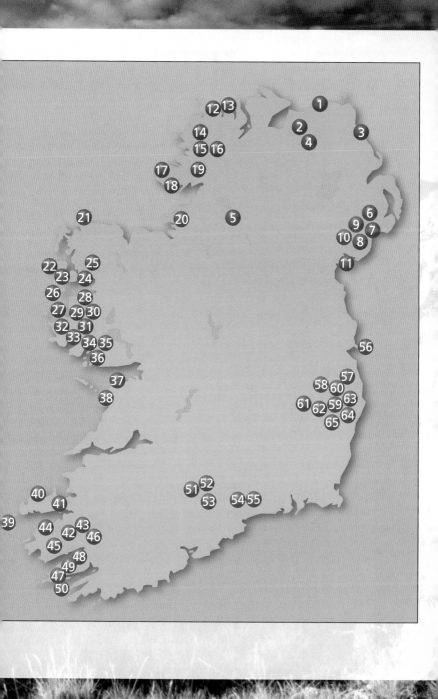

Quick Reference Route Table

No.	Walk Name	Category
1	Causeway Coast Path	Coastal Path
2	Binevenagh Cliffs	Hillwalk
3	The Antrim Hills	Hillwalk
4	Sawel and Dart	Hillwalk
5	Cuilcagh	Hillwalk
6	Slieve Meelmore and Slieve Meelbeg	Hillwalk
7	Slieve Donard	Hillwalk
8	Slieve Muck	Hillwalk
9	Slieve Bearnagh and the Silent Valley	Hillwalk
10	The Binnians	Hillwalk
11	Slieve Foye	Hillwalk
12	Melmore Head	Coastal Hillwalk
13	Muckish	Hillwalk
14	Errigal	Hillwalk
15	Slieve Snaght and the Poisoned Glen	Hillwalk
16	Glenveagh and Farscallop	Valley Path and Hillwalk
17	Glencolmcille Circuit	Coastal Hillwalk
18	Slieve League Traverse	Hillwalk
19	Lavagh Beg and Lavagh More	Hillwalk
20	Benbulbin and Benwiskin	Hillwalk
21	Benwee Head	Coastal Hillwalk
22	Achill Head and Croaghaun	Coastal Hillwalk
23	Minaun Heights	Coastal Hillwalk
24	Glendahurk Horseshoe	Hillwalk
25	Nephin	Hillwalk
26	Clare Island	Coastal Hillwalk
27	Inishturk	Coastal Hillwalk
28	Croagh Patrick	Hillwalk
29	Mweelrea	Hillwalk
30	Sheeffry Traverse	Hillwalk
31	Ben Creggan and Ben Gorm	Hillwalk
32	Diamond Hill	Mountain Path
33	Glencorbet Horseshoe	Hillwalk

Quick Reference Route Table *(cont'd)*

No.	Walk Name	Category
34	Glencoaghan Horseshoe	Hillwalk
35	Central Maumturks – North	Hillwalk
36	Central Maumturks – South	Hillwalk
37	Black Head	Hillwalk
38	Cliffs of Moher Coastal Path	Coastal Path
39	Great Blasket Island	Coastal Hillwalk
40	Brandon Mountain	Hillwalk
41	Slieve Mish Circuit	Hillwalk
42	Coomloughra Horseshoe	Hillwalk
43	The Reeks Ridge	Hillwalk
44	Coomasaharn	Hillwalk
45	Gearhameen Horseshoe	Hillwalk
46	Torc Mountain	Mountain Path
47	Dursey Island	Coastal Hillwalk
48	Cummeengeera Horseshoe	Hillwalk
49	Hungry Hill	Hillwalk
50	The Sheep's Head	Coastal Path
51	Galtymore	Hillwalk
52	Lough Muskry Circuit	Hillwalk
53	Knockmealdown Circuit	Hillwalk
54	Nire Valley Coums	Hillwalk
55	Coumshingaun	Hillwalk
56	Howth Cliff Path	Coastal Path
57	Great Sugar Loaf	Hillwalk
58	Mullaghcleevaun	Hillwalk
59	Luggala and Knocknacloghoge	Hillwalk
60	Djouce and War Hill	Hillwalk
61	Tonelagee	Hillwalk
62	Scarr and Kanturk	Hillwalk
63	Camaderry Circuit	Hillwalk
64	The Spinc Loop	Mountain Path
65	Lugnaquilla	Hillwalk

Grade	Distance	Ascent	Time	Page
5	16km	1,500m	8–9 hours	123
4	14km	810m	5–6 hours	127
4	13km	830m	5–6 hours	130
4	14.5km	410m	4½–5½ hours	133
2	13km	240m	3½–4½ hours	136
3	9km	450m	3–3½ hours	139
5	10km	1,000m	4½–5½ hours	142
4	11km	900m	4½–5½ hours	145
5	13.5km	1,200m	6–7 hours	148
5	12km	1,100m	6–7 hours	151
4	11.5km	800m	4½–5½ hours	154
4	10km	750m	4½–5½ hours	157
3	8km	490m	3–4 hours	160
3	11.5km	410m	3½–4½ hours	163
4	11km	900m	4½–5½ hours	166
4	9km	710m	3½–4½ hours	170
3	12.5km	320m	3½–4½ hours	173
5	12km	1,020m	5–6 hours	176
4	13km	730m	4½–5½ hours	179
4	11km	830m	4–5 hours	182
4	15.5km	800m	5–6 hours	186
5	8km	650m	3½–4 hours	189
2	10km	240m	3–3½ hours	192
3	5km	380m	2–2½ hours	195
4	8.5km	570m	3–4 hours	199
4	12km	780m	4½–5½ hours	202
4	14km	660m	4½–5½ hours	205
4	8km	490m	3–4 hours	209
4	14km	540m	4½–5½ hours	212
4	13km	630m	4½–5½ hours	215
3	11.5km	400m	3½–4 hours	218
4	13km	800m	5–6 hours	221

Beside a bog pool on the ridge between Minnaunmore and Benbaun. Twelve Bens, Connemara.

Introduction

Selecting the best walks in Ireland is an unenviable task. At first glance, sixty-five routes might seem like a generous figure, but once you consider the details of which trips to include, it soon becomes clear it is not nearly high enough. The problem is that Ireland is so well endowed with quality walks, making a narrow selection is nearly impossible.

The main criterion for inclusion in this guide is wild, dramatic scenery: high peaks, chiselled ridges and unspoilt coastline. Ireland boasts a wide variety of such landscapes and all are ripe for exploration. Yet it comes as no surprise that many of these places lie far off the beaten track. This, to me, is a bonus; my favourite sort of walking takes me to places I cannot access any other way than by foot. When the road ends, that is when I am inspired to head off with my backpack. And the sense of fulfilment that comes from discovering these hidden treasures stays with you long after you have returned home.

My hope is that whether you are an Irish native or a visitor to the country, you will be able to use this guide to reach the same wild places I have, and be rewarded for your effort by the same wonderful views and sense of achievement. You too can experience the natural high of standing on a lofty summit, miles from civilisation, and drinking in the incredible panorama at your feet.

By selecting only those routes that have most inspired me, I am aiming this guidebook at like-minded walkers. So to get the most from the book, you will need to know how to read a map and be confident across open ground. That is not to say that all the routes are technically demanding or especially long. There is a wide variety of trips lasting from two to eight hours, reflecting the diverse nature of the country's terrain.

Routes have been selected according to practical criteria too: circular routes have been prioritised over linear ones, and car parking and access issues have been carefully considered. The aim is to make it as easy as possible for you to identify a route that appeals to you, travel there, and then complete the walk in confidence. Of course, there is no legislating for those unforeseen events that may occur once you are out – least of all the weather – but such unpredictability is part of being close to nature, and one of the pleasures of walking in Ireland. Overall, I hope this book allows you to discover more about the country's wild and beautiful places, and that you get as much enjoyment from walking these routes as I do.

The Irish Landscape

Ireland is a small country, measuring just 486km long and 275km wide. Yet its compact form is an advantage in terms of getting around, and its diminutive size certainly should not be mistaken for a lack of topographical diversity. Within these narrow boundaries lies an impressive array of different landscapes.

The country's coastline stretches for an incredible 5,631km, and in some places is so indented and convoluted it provides a lesson in fractal geometry. The coast is sometimes low-lying and hospitable, with long, golden beaches and enclosed sandy coves. At other times it is wild and inaccessible, with sheer cliffs and thrusting headlands stretching unbroken for miles with just the waves and seabirds as their witness.

The land itself is relatively flat and fertile in the centre, with numerous mountain chains scattered around the periphery. All the country's most notable ranges – the Wicklow Mountains, the MacGillycuddy's Reeks, the Twelve Bens, the Derryveagh Mountains and the Mourne Mountains – lie in close proximity to the sea. The advantage of this for walkers is that summit views tend to encompass long stretches of coastline as well as neighbouring peaks, further enhancing their impact and variety.

The country has a total of fourteen mountains over 900m high, and 268 hills over 600m high. 'Mountain' is of course a relative term – at 1,039m high, Ireland's highest peak, Carrauntoohil, would not even register as a landmark in some countries. Yet many of the country's upland walks start from sea level, and it is not uncommon for a route to include 1,000m or more of vertical ascent: a respectable day's toil no matter where you are in the world.

Ireland's mountains owe much of their present form to the last ice age, which ended some 10,000 years ago. Prior to this almost the entire country was covered in ice, and the erosive forces of the great glaciers can be seen best in the mountains. The U-shaped valleys, deep-sided corries and sharp arêtes that now characterise the country's peaks are all direct results of the gouging flow of the ice.

First-time visitors to Ireland are often surprised by the lack of trees covering the summits, and most open ground is indeed bereft of vegetation more than ankle high. The country's long history of forest clearance stretches back to Neolithic times (around 3,000 BC), and native broadleaf woods are now a precious commodity. The occasional pocket of ancient woodland does still exist, but managed plantations of imported pine are much more common. Yet even taking the new plantations into account, Ireland remains one of the least forested countries in Europe, with just 10 per cent of its surface covered by trees. From a walking perspective, the absence of upland vegetation is just another factor that enhances the frequent, far-reaching views.

The felling of the trees also encouraged the formation of another dominant feature of the Irish landscape: bogland. Bog is made up of accumulations of decayed plant material, and it was once so extensive it covered a fifth of the county. Many of Ireland's mountains are still protected by swathes of bog, particularly in Connemara, Mayo and Donegal. Bogland makes for an arduous walking surface, and brave adventurers should be prepared for slow, wet and energy-sapping progress. Needless to say, the routes selected here have been designed to minimise the amount of bog-trotting required.

Walking Practicalities

Though Ireland has been split into two political jurisdictions since 1922, the border between Northern Ireland and the Republic is no longer of much practical significance for walkers. The main difference you will notice is using different money in the shops. In terms of climate, mapping, terrain, scenery and effort, the experience of walking is much the same north and south of the border.

More significant for walkers is the proximity of each walking area to the country's large urban centres. With both Dublin and Belfast – by far the largest cities in Ireland – located on the east coast, it comes as no surprise that the country's eastern ranges see the greatest number of people out exploring the hills. The Wicklow Mountains and the Mournes are particularly popular, and often described as the 'playgrounds' of the two cities. As a result of the frequent footfall, informal paths have formed across many of the high peaks in these areas.

Once you venture further west, the number of people you meet on a typical day out reduces significantly. Indeed, there are several shapely and immensely enjoyable ranges that come with a virtual guarantee of solitude, Mayo's Nephin Beg Mountains being a prime example. The term 'wild west' is still applicable to Ireland, and the sense of isolation can be a novel experience for anyone used to crowded trails elsewhere. In these more remote regions there is often little sign of previous footfall, and walkers must be entirely self-reliant.

A small number of the walks in this book follow signed footpaths, but the vast majority depend on the navigational skill of the individual walker. Even where informal paths have formed over popular peaks, these should not be relied on for navigational guidance. You will need to carry a map and compass for all the routes in the book, and know how to use them.

Access

The vast majority of land in Ireland is privately owned, and the public has no automatic right of access. Some recognised rights of way do exist, but these are not as numerous or as well protected in law as in many other European countries.

Generally speaking, Irish walks fall into four categories. First are the areas owned by public or semi-public bodies, such as the country's national parks and forests. Most of these areas have regulations that encourage access for walkers, and you can often walk unhindered within their boundaries. Second are areas of commonage, where ownership is shared amongst a number of local landowners. Again, walkers rarely experience any access restrictions here. Third are the signed walking routes, where local councils have negotiated with local landowners to establish an official footpath. There are often negotiations involved in setting up these routes, but once they have been established, you can walk with confidence in the knowledge that all access issues have been resolved. Finally there are the informal routes that cross private land. Many landowners happily tolerate public access and have permitted walkers to cross their land for many years, but others are not so welcoming, citing concerns over liability, trespass and damage to their property.

In the countryside, it is not always obvious whether a piece of land is privately owned, and what the wishes of the landowner are in terms of allowing access for walkers. The best advice is to do some research before you head out to check whether access is permitted, then to chat to locals once you arrive. Whatever the landowner's wishes, they must always be respected.

The advantage of using a guidebook like this is that all the routes here have already been checked in terms of access. Where a route crosses private land, however, in theory access can be withdrawn at any time, and it is not unheard of for previously established routes to be declared out of bounds. If you do encounter any access problems on the routes described in this book, please contact the publisher so we can address the issue in future editions.

Climate

Ireland enjoys a relatively mild climate all year round, with the prevailing winds coming from the west or southwest. Most rain falls as soon as the clouds meet land, so the east enjoys a slightly drier climate than the west. On average there are around 180 days of precipitation each year, and although the winter is wetter, there are still at least ten days of rain throughout Ireland during most of the summer months. The moral is that it is advisable to be prepared for showers even on apparently sunny days in the summer.

Prolonged spells of wet weather saturate the upland peat, making walking conditions boggy and arduous underfoot. In these conditions, it is best to wear gaiters and avoid routes that cross a lot of open moorland. Rainfall also affects the water levels of rivers, and can transform small mountain streams into raging torrents. River crossings can be very dangerous in spate conditions, and you should consider the effect of different water levels when planning your route.

The warmest months are July and August, when average daily temperatures reach 18 °C. However, many of the best outdoor experiences can be had on crisp, clear days in autumn, winter or spring. The coldest months are January and February, when daytime temperatures average around 6 °C, and night-time temperatures often drop below freezing. This is cold enough to freeze upland bog, and it is a great time to tackle the country's wetter walking routes. It is wonderful to skip across frozen peat, knowing you might be sinking knee-deep at any other time of the year.

Lowland areas rarely have more than a few days of snow each year. In the mountains, snow is more frequent and may linger for a week or more on the summits. It can cover paths, cairns and other navigational aids, and turn even moderately steep slopes into hazardous slides, so make sure you have the experience and equipment to cope with the conditions. Mountain access roads are often closed after heavy snowfalls too, so check the road conditions as well as the weather forecast before heading out in the winter.

Wind chill is perhaps the biggest danger to winter walkers once they are out in the elements. As a rule the air temperature drops 2–3 °C for every 300m of height gained. Add even a moderate wind chill factor and it soon becomes obvious that several layers of insulation might be needed to keep warm.

Another seasonal consideration for walkers is the amount of daylight. In mid December the sun rises around 8.40 a.m. and sets soon after 4 p.m., giving just seven and a half hours of daylight. By mid June, the sun sets at 10 p.m. and there are seventeen hours of daylight. It is quite possible to start an eight-hour walk at lunchtime and still finish with daylight to spare.

Maps

Ireland has a good range of high-quality outdoor mapping. The long-established standard reference for walkers in the Republic is the Ordnance Survey of Ireland (OSi) 1:50,000 *Discovery* series. In Northern Ireland, the equivalent is the Ordnance Survey of Northern Ireland (OSNI) 1:50,000 *Discoverer* range. Together, these maps cover the whole country, and some sheets are available with a waterproof covering. The general quality and accuracy of the mapping is very high, though it can lack detail in the placement of forest tracks and mountain paths.

Many of the country's most popular walking areas are also covered by smaller-scale mapping. These include four OSi 1:25,000 sheets and a range of OSNI 1:25,000 Activity Maps. Harvey also produce three 1:30,000 *Superwalker* maps for Ireland, while EastWest Mapping offer five 1:30,000 sheets covering the southeast of the country. The quality of cartography from both Harvey and EastWest Mapping is very high, and these maps often show paths, tracks and other details better than the OS equivalent.

It is worth noting that where different maps cover the same area, there are often small discrepancies between the information displayed, particularly in the spelling of place names and height of mountains. In this guide I have generally used the standard OS references unless there is good reason to do otherwise.

Useful Contacts

Listed below are the contact details of various service providers that might be of assistance to walkers.

Emergencies Dial 999 or 112 for all emergency services, including mountain rescue and coastguard.

Weather The Irish Meteorological Service provides a two-day online weather forecast for Ireland at www.met.ie. The BBC offers a five-day forecast for the UK and Ireland at www.bbc.co.uk/weather/2635167.

Maps To purchase walking maps from outside the region, go to the online shops at www.osi.ie, https://maps.osni.gov.uk, www.harveymaps.co.uk, or www.eastwestmapping.ie.

Forest Services Forestry plantations in the Republic of Ireland are overseen by Coillte. For more information about the facilities and walking trails in each forest, see www.coillteoutdoors.ie. Northern Ireland's forest parks are run by the Forest Service. For information about park facilities and walking trails, see www.dardni.gov.uk/forestservice.

Hillwalking Resource A great resource for Irish walkers is www.mountainviews.ie. This website provides practical details about all Ireland's mountains, with walkers' comments detailing different routes up each peak.

Northern Ireland Walk Directory If you want more information on walks in Northern Ireland, try www.walkni.com. The website has a searchable directory of hundreds of walking routes across the province.

Using This Guide

This guide consists of sixty-five route descriptions covering what I consider the best one-day walks in Ireland. All the routes were checked in 2013 and 2014, and descriptions were correct at that time.

Some of the walks are accessible by public transport, but you will need your own vehicle to reach the more remote excursions. The majority of the walks are circular in format, though there are also a few linear itineraries that use public transport to return to the starting point. Many of the routes are hill-walks, but these range from relatively short, signed loops to challenging trips across the open summits. Other routes are coastal circuits, and there are three routes on Atlantic islands that involve a ferry journey at the start and the end of the day.

Virtually all the walking takes place across open ground or along footpaths and tracks. Road walking has been kept to a bare minimum, and main roads have been avoided altogether.

Grading

Grades have been included to give an indication of the overall difficulty level, 1 being the easiest and 5 the hardest. None of the routes involves any technical difficulties that require rock-climbing skills.

Grade 1   Relatively short walks on well-graded, constructed paths. Surfaces are firm underfoot and little ascent or descent is involved. Routes are signposted throughout and there are no serious navigational difficulties.

Grade 2   Routes still follow signed paths, but these might not be constructed underfoot. Some sections cross rougher ground or open countryside. There are no serious navigational difficulties but routes may involve up to 400m of vertical ascent.

Grade 3   Walks in this category involve up to 500m of ascent. Terrain can be rough underfoot, though formal paths may still exist. Routes are generally not signed and navigation skills are required, but route finding should be relatively straightforward in good conditions. Most of the country's easy hill-walks fall into this category.

Grade 4   Longer mountain excursions with up to 1,000m of ascent. Ground can be very rough underfoot and any paths are informal in character. Navigational skills are required throughout and may be necessary to avoid natural hazards such as cliffs. Previous hillwalking experience is recommended.

Grade 5   The longest, most strenuous hill-walks fall into this category. Routes generally visit multiple summits, last at least five hours and involve over 1,000m of ascent. Some easy scrambling manoeuvres may be required on the most technical routes. Good stamina, solid navigational skills, and previous hillwalking experience are all prerequisites to complete these routes in safety.

Sketch Maps

Each walk description is accompanied by a sketch map, to help you locate the route on the relevant reference map. The major features of the landscape are marked, along with any smaller points that may help you follow the route. Please note that scales and bearings are indicative rather than precise, and sketch maps should not be relied on for navigational purposes.

Equipment

Boots are required for all walks unless the route description advises otherwise. Another general rule of walking in Ireland is that you should always be prepared for adverse weather. In the mountains in particular, warm and waterproof clothing is essential even on an apparently sunny day. Gaiters are advisable for cross-country routes after rain.

It is also assumed that the relevant map sheet and a compass will be carried on all routes. Mobile phone coverage is generally good on high ground around the country, but may be less reliable in remote valleys. Do not rely on being able to get a connection whenever you need it.

Responsible Walking

Some of the walking routes described in this book depend on the goodwill of landowners for their existence. Inconsiderate behaviour by walkers may lead to access being withdrawn and apparently established routes being lost. Damage to farm fences and walls, sheep-worrying dogs, inconsiderate parking and litter are some of the main reasons why walkers become unpopular with landowners.

Inconsiderate outdoor behaviour can also have a negative impact on the environment and on other people's enjoyment of the area. Leave No Trace Ireland is a network of organisations that promote responsible recreational use of the outdoors. They have designed a programme to help walkers and other outdoor enthusiasts understand the impact of their activities and to value the natural environment. For full details of the principles involved, please see www.leavenotraceireland.org.

Causeway Coast Path

This magnificent linear path takes you past the most celebrated stretch of coastline in Northern Ireland.

Grade:	2
Time:	5–6 hours
Distance:	15km (9½ miles)
Ascent:	200m (660ft)
Map:	Maps: OSNI 1:50,000 sheet 5, or OSNI 1:25,000 *Causeway Coast and Rathlin Island* or *Glens of Antrim*.

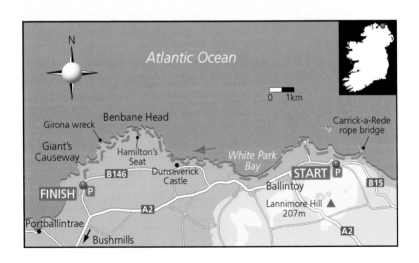

Start & Finish: The route starts at the parking area for Carrick-a-Rede rope bridge (grid reference: D052448). The site is signed from the B12 just east of Ballintoy. The walk finishes at the car park for the Giant's Causeway (grid reference: C945439). The causeway is situated along the B146, around 3km north of Bushmills.

The basalt columns of the Giant's Causeway are visited on the route.

This varied and highly enjoyable route explores the numerous natural attractions of the north Antrim coast. The 40,000 hexagonal rocks of the Giant's Causeway form perhaps the most famous feature of the walk, but the whole coastline is so striking it is protected as an Area of Outstanding Natural Beauty.

The route described here follows the best section of the two-day Causeway Coast Way. It starts at the thrilling Carrick-a-Rede rope bridge and traces the shoreline west past sandy beaches, secluded harbours, sheer cliff tops and historic landmarks. Despite its linear format, return transport is not a problem. The walk's start and the finish points are linked via frequent bus services – use the Ulsterbus Causeway Rambler shuttle service during the summer, and the Antrim Coaster service at other times of the year.

The path is signed throughout, and frequent access points mean you can split it into sections to suit your own preferences. Note, however, that the shoreline at either end of White Park Bay is impassable at high tide, so make sure to check the tide times before you set out. There is also a charge for visiting the rope bridge at the start of the walk, and for parking at the Giant's Causeway at the end.

The Walk

If this is your first time visiting Carrick-a-Rede, a trip across the thrilling 20m-long rope bridge is highly recommended. Pay your dues at the entrance kiosk and follow a constructed gravel pathway east from the car park. This initial side trip adds 2km to the day's total.

Return to the car park and begin the route itself. Follow the path west along the cliff top, with Rathlin Island and Scotland's Mull of Kintyre both visible across the sea. Join a minor road and turn right, descending to the quiet, picturesque harbour at Ballintoy. The road ends here, but the route continues west along a track, then a footpath. Pass a series of stacks and islands to reach the top of a stone beach. A brief boulder hop around the base of a cliff now brings you onto the 2km sweep of golden sand at White Park Bay.

Cross the beach to the cliffs at its western end. Here you have to clamber across more boulders to reach Portbradden, an idyllic collection of houses fronted by a small harbour. St Gobban's Church lies beside the second house; it is no larger than a garden shed and holds the accolade of smallest church in Ireland.

Continue through a natural rock arch and follow the path around Gid Point, crossing a mixture of rock and grass as you trace the indented coastline to Dunseverick. Several more stiles need to be crossed on this 2km stretch, which ends at the ruins of sixteenth-century Dunseverick Castle.

The grassy path continues northwest from here, climbing towards Benbane Head and Hamilton's Seat, the highest part of the route. You are now tracing the cliff line some 100m above the ocean and there are wonderful views west along the rugged coastline. Midway between Hamilton's Seat and the Giant's Causeway you come to Plaskin Head. This marks the final resting place of the *Girona*, the most famous ship of the ill-fated 1588 Spanish Armada.

It is not long now before you arrive at the Giant's Causeway. If you do not want to visit the site itself, continue along the cliff path to the visitor centre. Alternatively, a steep descent down the Shepherd's Steps will bring you to the basalt columns at the shore. Legend dictates that the Irish giant Fionn Mac Cumhaill built the causeway as part of a bridge over to Scotland. However, scientists maintain the hexagonal structures were created by cooling lava flows around 60 million years ago.

To finish, follow the 1km-long tarmac driveway from the causeway to the visitor centre, which is situated at the top of the hill to the west.

ROUTE 2:
Binevenagh Cliffs

This short circuit explores the cliffs and pinnacles of one of the most fascinating landscapes in the north.

Grade:	3
Time:	2–2½ hours
Distance:	6.5km (4 miles)
Ascent:	200m (660ft)
Map:	OSNI 1:50,000 sheet 4.

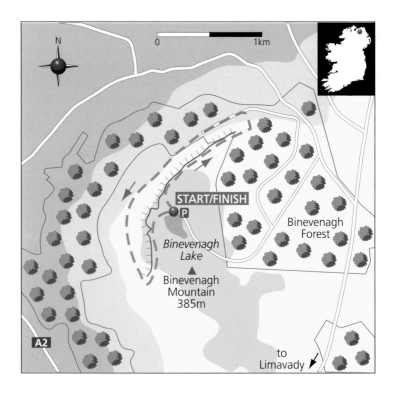

N

0   1km

START/FINISH
P

Binevenagh Forest

Binevenagh Lake

▲
Binevenagh Mountain
385m

A2

to Limavady

Walker dwarfed beneath the Binevenagh cliffs.

Start & Finish: The circuit starts and finishes at a car park beside Binevenagh Lake, at the top of the cliffs (grid reference: C691308). From Limavady, take the A2 north to Artikelly, then continue east on the B201 towards Coleraine. Turn left 2km east of Artikelly, then turn left again after 5km, following signs for Binevenagh Forest. The forest entrance is located on the left 1km further on. Follow the track uphill to reach the car park at the end of the road.

The Binevenagh cliffs stand sentinel above the Magilligan lowlands of northern County Derry. Cutting into the northern slopes of Binevenagh Mountain, this dramatic basalt escarpment has a vertical drop of more than 100m and dominates the landscape for miles around.

The cliffs and their attendant stacks and pinnacles make an intriguing place to explore. The precipice harbours both Arctic-alpine and coastal flora, and has been classified an Area of Special Scientific Interest. The rock itself was created by ancient lava flows and invites inevitable comparison with the more famous basalt formations of the Giant's Causeway, 30km away to the east.

This route makes a circuit around the main escarpment, exploring the rock walls from above and below. Though it is relatively short, the quality of the scenery means it is recommended for everyone. Navigation is relatively straightforward, with stiles and informal footpaths to ease your progress.

However, there is no avoiding the fact that half the walk takes place beside a sheer drop; please exercise due care and attention near the cliff edge.

The Walk

From the car park, head towards the cliffs on a grassy path signed by an old marker post. Keep right at a fork and follow the trail to the cliff edge, where you are met by a fantastic view. The farmland beneath you is, in fact, the largest coastal plain in Ireland, backed by the waters of Lough Foyle and the hills of Inishowen.

Follow the path northeast along the cliff top to the edge of a forest. Here you veer right, away from the cliff. Many of the trees have been felled in this area, and the path descends several awkward steps as it negotiates the exposed roots. Console yourself with the thought that this is the roughest terrain of the route and will soon be behind you. Follow the trail as it swings left into the trees, then zigzags down through the forest, still descending a steep slope that can be muddy after rain.

At the bottom of the slope, join a gravel vehicle track and turn left. When the track comes to an end, continue ahead on a small footpath and cross a stile beside a metal gate. You are now out into the open, directly beneath the Binevenagh cliffs.

Follow a faint path along the right-hand side of the field. When the trees fall away to your right, begin to traverse across the field to the left, climbing very gradually towards the base of the rocky escarpment. Along the way you will need to cross several more fences, each of which is bridged by a wooden stile. The path eventually becomes lost in the grass, though the general line of the route is indicated by the stiles.

Towards the centre of the cliffs a steep gully cuts down the precipice. Beyond this the ground begins to undulate through a series of hummocks. Keep climbing, drawing gradually closer to the base of the cliffs. Two distinct waves of rock now lie to your left, the nearer stacks and having broken off the main escarpment.

Continue ahead, now passing between several sharp hummocks. Eventually you will see a distinctive tooth of rock lying just beneath the main precipice, with a grassy ramp to its left. The path consolidates again near the base of this ramp and a steady climb brings you up the slope to the top of the cliffs.

Veer left as you reach the top of the escarpment and begin to trace the cliff line north. Keep climbing gently over the grassy slope and pass through a metal gate in a fence. Soon after this the ascent eases and Binevenagh Lake comes into sight ahead. Continue along the edge of the precipice until you are forced right by the lip of a gully. Follow the path to the lakeshore, then turn left across the concrete outlet dam. A final track leads the last few metres back to the car park.

ROUTE 3:
The Antrim Hills

A linear route across the Glens of Antrim, following an undulating ridgeline with fine coastal views.

Grade:	3
Time:	5½–6½ hours
Distance:	21km (13 miles)
Ascent:	480m (1,575ft)
Map:	OSNI 1:50,000 sheet 9, or OSNI 1:25,000 *Glens of Antrim*.

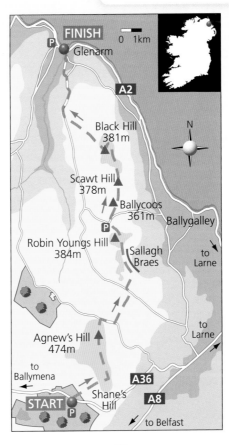

Start & Finish: The route starts from a car park in Ballyboley Forest on Shane's Hill (grid reference: J314992). The car park is marked by a route information board, and is situated on the southern side of the A36 Larne–Ballymena road, around 10km west of Larne and 21km east of Ballymena.

The route ends at a seafront car park in Glenarm village, on the A2 Larne–Carnlough road (grid reference: D310154).

This is probably the most enjoyable upland route in the Antrim Hills, with firm terrain, dramatic natural landforms and fantastic views from start to finish. The most striking formation is Sallagh Braes, a semicircular basalt escarpment that was created when glacial ice cut into unstable slopes and caused a massive landslip, leaving the vertical cliffs 2km long and 100m high that are visible today.

The route traverses a series of summits between 300m and 474m high. It follows the most scenic part of the two-day Antrim Hills Way, and is furnished with frequent stiles and waymarking posts. Much of the time is spent on faint paths across open terrain, and though route finding is relatively simple in good conditions, full navigation skills are required in bad weather.

If you have two vehicles, it is possible to avoid the final 3km of tarmac by parking on wide verges on the road above Glenarm. If not, consider taking the Glenarm–Larne and Larne–Ballymena buses to transport yourself between start and finish. The route can also be split into shorter sections by starting and finishing at the car park between Ballycoos and Robin Youngs Hill.

The Walk

From Shane's Hill car park, cross the road and join a grassy footpath beside a route signpost. Follow the path along a firebreak in the forest and cross a stile to reach open peat moorland.

The cairn that marks the southern summit of Agnew's Hill is now visible to the northeast. Head directly towards the cairn, climbing gradually over rough tussock grass. Cross two tracks and a stile to reach the summit itself. You are rewarded with your first real views, which include the Belfast Hills, the Mourne Mountains, the Sperrins and Scotland. It is a wonderful panorama, and one that stays with you for the duration of the route.

Turn left at the cairn and descend slightly, then begin the steady ascent to the higher, northern peak. The summit cairn, and highest point of the route at 474m, lies at the far edge of the plateau.

When you are ready to descend, follow the marker posts to a stile, then turn right beside a fence. Continue downhill to meet a road, then head

Sheep grazing beneath Robin Youngs Hill.

right along the tarmac for almost 1km. Cross a stile on the left, then follow the path over a field and cross a stream above an artificial lough. Here you join a grassy track bound by high stone walls, which brings you to another minor road.

Turn left along the road for 120m, then turn right. A series of stiles leads across the fields to heathery ground above Sallagh Braes. Follow a fence around the lip of this escarpment, with gullies allowing the occasional glimpse into the void below. The airy sensation and the view over the curving cliffs make this a memorable piece of walking.

The path now climbs over the shoulder of Robin Youngs Hill, then descends over a stony track and cropped grass to reach a car park. Cross the road here, and climb along the right side of a field to the summit of Ballycoos. A gradual descent and ascent then brings you to Scawt Hill. Continue in the same vein across a series of grassy undulations, keeping to the high ground near the eastern edge of the plateau. The coastal views remain impressive throughout, with the rocky outcrops of the Maidens, or Hulin Rocks, visible out to sea.

The path eventually swings west across rougher ground to reach the trig point at the summit of Black Hill. This marks the start of a diagonal descent northwest off the plateau. Follow the marker posts down through the fields and across several rocky hummocks. Eventually you meet a stone wall at the right side of a field and descend through gorse bushes to a road.

Turn right along the road and follow the tarmac for almost 2km, then turn left onto a smaller road. You arrive at the top of Altmore Street in Glenarm village roughly 1km later. Follow the street to a T-junction with the A2, then turn left for 200m to finish at the village's seafront car park.

Sawel and Dart

A rugged but rewarding mountain circuit over the highest peak in the Sperrin Mountains.

Grade:	4
Time:	5–6 hours
Distance:	14km (8½ miles)
Ascent:	650m (2,100ft)
Map:	OSNI 1:50,000 sheet 13, or OSNI 1:25,000 Activity Map *Sperrins*.

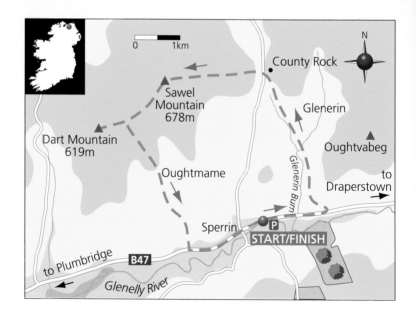

Start & Finish: The route starts and finishes at a lay-by along the B47 in the Glenelly Valley (grid reference: H639944). The lay-by is located around 500m east of Sperrin village crossroads, on the southern side of the road. There is parking space for at least eight vehicles.

Dart (left) and Sawel (right) rising above the Glenelly Valley.

This circuit explores the very heart of the Sperrin Mountains, Northern Ireland's second highest mountain group. The range gets its name from the Irish *Cnoc Speirín*, meaning 'The Pointed Hills'. The label is something of a misnomer, however, because there are no airy ridges or plunging cliffs here, just rounded, peat-covered slopes. But pick a good day for your walk, when the ground is dry and the views are at their best, and you will find there is no better way to appreciate the landscape of counties Derry and Tyrone.

This route is the region's classic upland outing. It begins by climbing Sawel Mountain, the highest point of the range at 678m. Also on the itinerary is neighbouring Dart Mountain (619m), whose exposed rock outcrops make it the most distinctive summit in the chain. Tracks ease your progress on the approach and descent routes but rough, mountainous terrain must be negotiated between the two summits. A series of fences provides directional guidance, but navigational skills are required in bad weather. The route also includes 3.5km of road walking, which can be avoided if you have two vehicles or a bike.

The Walk

From the lay-by, head east along the B47. Though traffic is not generally heavy, vehicles do travel quickly along this road, so please take care. After 500m the road drops steeply to cross Glenerin Bridge, then climbs past a small conifer plantation. Next on the left is a farm, and 150m beyond this is a track and metal gate, set at an angle to the road.

Pass through the gate and begin climbing along the track. The track is overgrown with tussock grass for the first couple of kilometres, through it is still obvious enough to follow. Climb gradually around the slopes of Oughtvabeg, passing through several more gates on the way.

After 2km the track descends slightly across the Glenerin Burn, located near a farm shed. Either cross the stream directly, or detour 20m and cross a concrete bridge to reach a metal gate on the other side. The gate gives access to a firmer, more established track. Follow this gradually uphill, with the summits of Sawel and Dart now both visible to the east. Continue along the track until you reach the road over Sawel Pass. Cross the tarmac, veering 10m to the left to avoid crossing any fences.

This is where the real hillwalking begins; you now have 360 vertical metres to climb in a little over 2km. Begin by following the fence uphill to the west, crossing rough grass interspersed with occasional wet patches. Where a fence crosses your line of travel, cross the fence on your right and continue climbing. The wire acts as a guide rail, leading you virtually all the way to the summit of Sawel. Where it finally veers away to the left, continue ahead for another 100m to reach the trig point itself.

It is worth taking some time here to appreciate the views. The panorama extends for 360°, taking in most of Northern Ireland as well as counties Donegal and Sligo. There is also a clear view of the next part of the route to Dart Mountain. Begin by descending southwest, again following the right side of a fence. The peat hags in the col are not as awkward as they appear, and another steady ascent brings you past the rock outcrops that decorate the top of Dart Mountain. As before, you must leave the fence for the final few metres to the large summit cairn.

When you are ready to descend, retrace your steps east until you reach a fence junction. Now turn south and follow along the left side of another fence, heading down the shoulder between Garvegh Burn and Oughtmane Burn. A long, gradual descent over rough grass brings you to another boundary. Pass through a gate on the left, beside a small conifer plantation. Continue directly ahead from the gate, where a track materialises underfoot. This soon consolidates into a charming green lane; follow this down through several gates to reach the B47. Turn left here and complete the final 2km along the road to the start.

ROUTE 5:
Cuilcagh

Two waymarked trails cross a sea of bog and converge at the highest point in County Fermanagh.

Grade:	4
Time:	5½–6½ hours
Distance:	16km (10 miles)
Ascent:	540m (1,770ft)
Map:	Map: OSNI 1:50,000 sheet 26

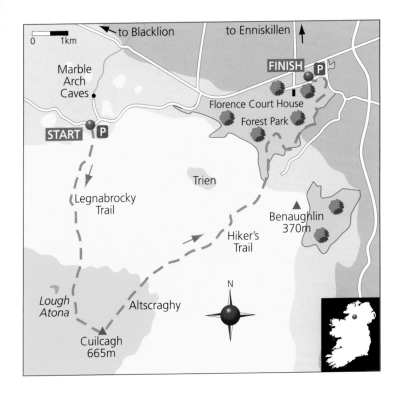

Start & Finish: The route starts at the car park for Cuilcagh Mountain Park (grid reference: H121335). To reach the area, follow signs for Marble Arch Caves from the A4/N16 Enniskillen–Blacklion road. The car park is located 300m west of the entrance to Marble Arch.

The route finishes at the Forest Service car park inside Florence Court estate (grid reference: H183347). Florence Court is also well signed from the A4/N16 Enniskillen–Blacklion road.

Once inside the entry gate, follow the driveway for 300m then turn left into the forest service car park, which is marked by an information panel for the Cuilcagh Way.

Cuilcagh Mountain (665m) straddles the border of counties Fermanagh and Cavan. A long, flat-topped peak flanked by a band of steep cliffs, it forms an isolated island in a sea of bog. The northern slopes of the mountain are complex enough to have been designated a European Geopark.

This route follows two marked walking paths over Cuilcagh, using the Legnabrocky Trail on the approach and the Hiker's Trail on the descent. Of the two routes, the Legnabrocky Trail is far easier because it uses a gravel track and wooden boardwalk to reach the mountain. The Hiker's Trail is unsurfaced and spends much of its time crossing wet blanket bog. The entire route is marked with frequent yellow-topped posts, and forms part of the two-day Cuilcagh Way.

If you have only one vehicle or have an aversion to bog, consider an out-and-back ascent via the Legnabrocky Trail.

The Walk

Walk to the southwestern corner of the car park and cross a stile beside a wooden gate. To the right of the stile is Monastir Sink, a collapsed cavern with an underground river that links to Marble Arch Caves.

Now head south along a gravel track, passing through limestone meadows and crossing a stone bridge and several more stiles. The landscape soon changes to blanket bog but the track continues on, undulating towards Cuilcagh for some 4km. Where the track ends, a section of wooden boardwalk continues ahead, providing an easy walking surface over the wet ground below. You arrive at the base of Cuilcagh just east of Lough Atona. Climb a wooden staircase that ascends the steep flanks of the mountain, enjoying fine views across the lake as you gain height.

The walkway deposits you at the edge of the summit plateau, where you have a choice of routes. The most impressive cliffs are situated to the west, above Lough Atona, and it is well worth turning right and making

Looking over Lough Atona from Cuilcagh's northern cliffs.

the 1km detour to visit these. Alternatively, to continue directly to the summit, keep to the marked trail and head east across the rock-strewn plateau on a rough footpath.

The official summit lies at the eastern tip of the mountain. Here, a concrete trig point sits atop a large stone cairn, which is actually the remains of a burial mound dating from the Bronze Age (2500–500 BC). Wide-ranging views encompass much of counties Fermanagh, Cavan and Leitrim.

If you are continuing onto the Hiker's Trail, walk 30m northeast from the summit cairn, to the edge of the plateau. Now descend diagonally left, beneath a band of rock, and cross a stile. A steep descent brings you down the grassy slope to base of the mountain. The waymarking posts now lead northeast, heading between the hills of Trien and Benaughlin in the distance. You have almost 5km of undulating bog to cross, and the ground is consistently wet underfoot. Remind yourself that blanket bog is a rare and precious habitat despite its inconveniences as a walking surface.

The landscape begins to change as you approach Benaughlin. Farm buildings can be seen to the right as you cross from moorland to grassy meadows. Follow the posts to the edge of Florence Court Forest and cross a wooden stile marked for the Hiker's Trail.

The path now descends along the edge of a forest and joins a vehicle track. Follow this down through several sweeping bends to a T-junction. Turn right here and pass through Glen Wood Nature Reserve, partly following the wooded banks of the beautiful Finglass River. The waymarkers now direct you along the edge of a field, with the eighteenth-century Florence Court House sitting commandingly atop a rise to the left.

Cross a river via a wooden bridge and keep left at the next three junctions. You now pass Ladies Well and reach the estate's main entrance driveway. Cross over the road and follow a final section of path to the finish at the forest service car park.

Slieve Meelmore and Slieve Meelbeg

A fine circuit across two conical summits in the northwestern corner of the Mourne Mountains.

Grade:	4
Time:	4–5 hours
Distance:	11km (7 miles)
Ascent:	685m (2,250ft)
Map:	OSNI 1:50,000 sheet 29, or OSNI 1:25,000 *The Mournes*.

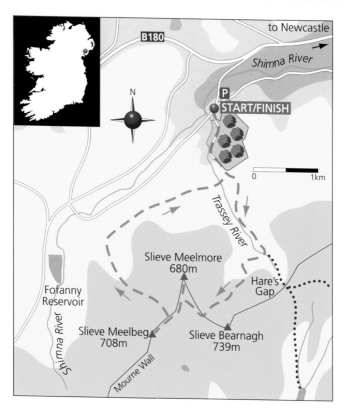

Start & Finish: The circuit starts and finishes at the Trassey Track car park, around 9km west of Newcastle (grid reference: J312314). From Newcastle, head west to Bryansford, then turn left onto the B180 towards Hilltown. After 4km, turn left onto a minor road. The car park is situated on the left around 1.5km later.

The Mourne Mountains are Northern's Ireland's premier mountain range, encompassing a tight cluster of granite peaks, seven of which reach above 700m high. This circuit takes you across Slieve Meelmore (680m) and Slieve Meelbeg (708m), two fine summits at the northwestern corner of the range.

Besides providing a highly enjoyable and compact walking circuit, these two mountains also make superlative vantage points. Summit views sweep across the entire Mourne range, encompassing almost all of its assembled peaks as well as the intervening loughs and reservoirs.

The route largely follows tracks and well-trodden mountain paths, and includes a return section along the Mourne Way. This, combined with the presence of the Mourne Wall over the high ground, means route finding is a relatively simple matter. If you want to extend the circuit, begin by following the Trassey Track to Hare's Gap and add an ascent of Slieve Bearnagh.

The Walk

From the entrance to the car park, turn left and walk along the road for 100m. This brings you to the start of a gravel track, marked with an information board for the Trassey Track. Turn left and cross the stile beside the entrance gate, then begin to follow the track south.

Pass two further gates with adjacent stiles to reach open terrain at the foot of the Mourne Mountains. At the final gate, a stone wall can be seen extending west around the base of Slieve Meelmore. This wall marks the line of the Mourne Way, and your return route.

For now, continue south along the Trassey Track, climbing through a couple of gentle switchbacks. After 1.5km you reach a junction beneath the northern slopes of Slieve Bearnagh. Turn right here and follow a subsidiary track past a small quarry. Where the vehicle track ends, a narrow footpath continues ahead, climbing along the banks of a mountain stream.

As you gain height, the unmistakable line of the Mourne Wall appears at the top of the gap. The final section of path has been constructed with granite slabs, providing an easier walking surface underfoot. Once at the col, cross the large wooden stile that spans the wall and turn right. Two walls make their way up Slieve Meelmore from this point: a new wall on the right and an older wall (semi-ruined at the bottom) on the left. The easiest line of ascent can be found beside the old wall.

39

Nearing the summit of Slieve Meelbeg in winter.

Climb steeply to the top of the wall and turn right. Now trace another short section of wall to reach the conspicuous stone shelter, built in 1921, that adorns the summit of Slieve Meelmore. A wooden stile allows you to cross the wall and appreciate the view in all directions. On a clear day Cave Hill is visible above Belfast city to the north, while Lambay Island, northeast of Dublin, can be seen beyond the Silent Valley Reservoir to the south.

Retrace your steps south from the summit, keeping the wall on your right. Descend through a col and then make the 100m climb to Slieve Meelbeg. Though this summit is marginally higher than Slieve Meelmore, it is far less distinctive, marked only by a slight bend in the wall and a small cairn. The new vantage point allows Spelga reservoir and dam to come into view to the west.

From Slieve Meelbeg, return northeast along the wall to the col beneath Slieve Meelmore. Now cross a wooden stile over the wall and begin to descend northwest down the centre of the valley beyond. Head down the left bank of a stream, with the grassy terrain merging into a stone track towards the bottom of the slope. Follow the track to a junction with the Mourne Way. Turn right along this footpath, cross the stream and pick up the line of a boundary wall. Follow the path along the wall for almost 2km, passing around the northwestern base of Slieve Meelmore.

Several small streams are crossed before the path brings you back to the Trassey Track. Turn left onto the track and retrace your initial steps back to the car park.

Slieve Donard

A highly enjoyable circular route over the highest mountain in Northern Ireland. The classic hill-walk in the province.

Grade:	4
Time:	4–5 hours
Distance:	9km (5½ miles)
Ascent:	850m (2,800ft)
Map:	OSNI 1:50,000 sheet 29, or OSNI 1:25,000 *The Mournes*.

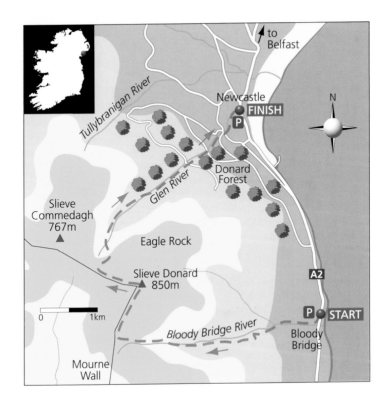

View across the Mourne Mountains from the top of Slieve Donard

Start & Finish: The walk starts at the Bloody Bridge car park, 3km south of Newcastle on the A2 to Kilkeel (grid reference: J388271). It finishes at the large parking area for Donard Park at the southern end of Newcastle town (grid reference: J375305).

At 850m, the summit of Slieve Donard is the highest point in the province of Ulster. It is also a supreme viewpoint on a clear day. The mountain towers over the town of Newcastle and its coastal location adds to its charm. Little wonder then that it is a veritable magnet for local and visiting hillwalkers alike.

Many walkers climb Donard from Newcastle, ascending along the Glen River Track and retracing their steps on the descent. This is a rather more interesting, almost circular, variation of that route, which approaches the mountain along the equally lovely Bloody Bridge River.

Route finding is relatively simple throughout, thanks to a series of maintained footpaths and the guidance of the Mourne Wall. However, the start and finish points are separated by 3.5km of road – a road that carries a lot of fast-moving traffic and does not make for pleasant walking. Unless you have two vehicles at your disposal, it is best to leave your car at Donard Park and arrange alternative transport to the start; consider taking either a local taxi or the No 37 Ulsterbus service.

The Walk

The Bloody Bridge footpath begins just across the road from the southern end of the car park. Pass through a narrow entrance gate and join the well-constructed stone path. The Bloody Bridge River, or the Mid-Pace River as it was once known, rushes over a series of rock slabs beside the path. Looking back downstream, there is a good view over the original Bloody Bridge. The name itself stems from gruesome events in 1641 when nine local Protestants and their minister were massacred at the bridge.

The path climbs along the right bank, becoming rougher as it progresses. After 1km you may want to cross the river and join a rough quarry track that lies just out of sight up to the left. Alternatively you can continue to pick your way along the river, crossing the stream where necessary. Both options involve 2km of steady ascent before you reach an old quarry.

Leave the quarry via a grassy track on the right and continue to climb to a broad col. Here the view suddenly opens out westwards across the wider Mournes, with the Annalong Valley immediately beneath you.

The col also marks your rendezvous with the Mourne Wall, which acts as your guide for the next part of the route. Turn right in front of the wall and follow the granite blocks directly up the slopes of Slieve Donard. The ascent is now steep and sustained; some 300m of altitude is gained in less than a kilometre. Fortunately, short grass underfoot makes for fairly easy progress.

The summit itself is marked by a stone tower and trig point, with a large summit cairn and a smaller one about 100m north that date from early Christian times. As you would expect, the views are magnificent. On a clear day you can survey the entire Mourne range, with Lough Neagh and the Sperrin Mountains to the northwest, and the Isle of Man visible across the Irish Sea.

The Mourne Wall turns sharply west at the summit, marking your line of descent. Drop steeply down to the col beneath Slieve Commedagh, where you must leave the wall behind. Turn right onto a path that descends down the centre of the valley to the northeast. The path is partially paved with stone slabs and while the first section is steep, the gradient soon eases. As you descend, the Glen River gathers force beside you, which you follow all the way to the end of the route.

Shortly before leaving the mountains you will notice a conspicuous beehive structure on the opposite side of the river. This is an old icehouse, used by the Slieve Donard Hotel before the advent of refrigeration. Now pass through a gate and enter Donard Wood, where you are immediately surrounded by a wonderful mixture of pine and deciduous trees.

Continue to follow the path as it descends along the tumbling falls of the Glen River, keeping to the left bank at the first bridge and crossing the river at two subsequent bridges. Finish by passing the grassy expanse of Donard Park to reach the car park.

Slieve Muck

A relatively straightforward mountain circuit that showcases the best views in the southern Mournes.

Grade:	4
Time:	4½–5½ hours
Distance:	13km (8 miles)
Ascent:	560m (1,840ft)
Map:	OSNI 1:50,000 sheet 29, or OSNI 1:25,000 *The Mournes*.

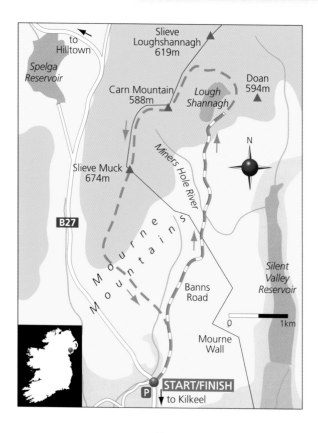

Start & Finish: The circuit starts and finishes at a car park at the bottom of the track known as the Banns Road (grid reference: J284214). The track begins beside The Gatekeeper's Lodge, and is situated along the B25, roughly 13km southeast of Hilltown and 7.5km north of Kilkeel.

Looking northeast from the slopes of Slieve Muck.

I f you are looking for a relatively easy hill-walk that shows the Mournes at their best, this could be the route for you. All the main peaks of the range can be seen from distinctive aspects, yet the 560m of ascent is so gradual it is barely noticeable. There is an enjoyable sense of calm around the route too – this region is remarkably quiet in comparison to some of the more renowned hillwalking areas in the northern and eastern parts of the range.

Besides the peaks themselves, the main focal point of the circuit is Lough Shannagh, the largest natural lake in the Mournes. Translating from the Irish as 'Lake of the Foxes', the lough fills a hollow dammed by glacial moraine.

Route finding is a relatively straightforward, thanks to a series of tracks and paths and the guidance of the Mourne Wall. However, there is a sting in the tail. The descent from Slieve Muck is steep, and care is needed to avoid the crags that guard much of the mountain's eastern flank. In good conditions it is simply a matter of taking your time to locate the best descent route, but in poor visibility solid navigation skills will be required.

The Walk

From the parking area, head northeast along the stone track known as the Banns Road. Soon you cross a stile beside a gate, and arrive out onto open mountain terrain. Slieve Muck now rises steeply to the northwest, and it is worth taking the time to locate your descent route down the mountain's southeastern tip for later on.

The track climbs gently beside the Yellow River for roughly 2km until it reaches the Mourne Wall, breached by another gate and stile. Cross the wall and before long you arrive at a small stone bridge over the Miner's Hole River. This tumbling stream is named in honour of the Cornish miners who once surveyed the area in the hope of extracting metallic ore from the famous Mourne granite.

Continue to follow the track all the way to Lough Shannagh. The lake is bordered by several sandy beaches, which provide a great place for a rest. Your next goal is the path that can be seen crossing the slope above the northeastern end of the lough. Follow a series of old concrete posts along the lake's eastern shore and cross the Shannagh River. A short, rough ascent brings you to the path itself. Now turn left and follow the trail towards the col between Carn Mountain and Slieve Loughshannagh.

At the col you meet the Mourne Wall again. Turn left and follow the wall up the slopes of Carn Mountain. Short grass makes for relatively easy progress all the way to the summit, where wonderful views encompass all the main peaks of the range to the northeast.

The summit of Carn Mountain is marked by a junction of walls. Turn right and follow the wall that descends west towards the col beneath Slieve Muck. Once at the col, veer south and begin the gradual ascent to Slieve Muck. The ground is now rougher underfoot, with tussock grass predominating.

The top of Slieve Muck is also marked by a junction of walls. Turn right here and cross a stile to reach the trig point that marks the official summit. The best views are now to the southwest, over Carlingford Lough and the outlying Mourne hills.

From the trig point, descend across open ground to reach a cairn that lies on top of a rise to the southwest. Continue past the cairn, keeping to the top of the main ridge across two subsidiary rises. Care is now needed to locate the correct descent route. Continue to the end of the main ridge, where the ground drops away steeply in all directions. Turn southeast here and pick your way carefully down the steep, grassy slope. The ground remains steep for 150m of vertical descent before easing off into the valley below.

Head for the point where the Yellow River meets a stone wall. Cross the river on stepping stones around 100m north of the wall. A short, boggy section brings you back to the Banns Road. Turn right along the track and retrace your initial steps back to the car park.

Slieve Bearnagh and the Silent Valley

A varied and immensely scenic circuit that makes a backdoor approach to the distinctive summit of Slieve Bearnagh.

Grade:	4
Time:	4½–5½ hours
Distance:	11km (7 miles)
Ascent:	850m (2,800ft)
Map:	OSNI 1:50,000 sheet 29, or OSNI 1:25,000 *The Mournes*.

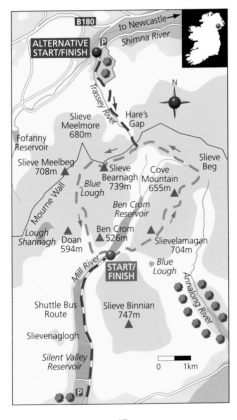

Start & Finish: The route starts and finishes beneath Ben Crom dam, around 12km north of Kilkeel (grid reference: J314254). Begin by heading to the Silent Valley Mountain Park, which is well signed from the A2 Newcastle–Kilkeel road. Park at a large car park beside the Silent Valley visitor centre. Entry to the park costs £4.50, and there is an additional charge of £1.40 for the shuttle bus, which carries you along the 4km of road to and from Ben Crom dam.

Alternatively, you can start for free at the Trassey Track car park (grid reference: J312314; see Slieve Meelmore & Slieve Meelbeg, p. 38, for full access details).

This route circles high above Ben Crom Reservoir as it explores the mountains around the head of the Silent Valley, in the very heart of the Mournes. The views are fantastic, but you will need to negotiate some steep ascents and rough terrain as you visit summits such as Slievelamagan (704m) and Slieve Bearnagh (739m). Navigation is helped in parts by footpaths and the Mourne Wall, but other sections cross open mountain slopes and you will have to rely on your own skills.

The advantage of starting at the Silent Valley Mountain Park is that you can explore the base of this famous valley as well as the peaks at its head. The area around the car park contains a visitor centre, café, several short, signed walks and various other recreational facilities. However, this start/finish point is best kept for the summer months, between May and September. During this period the grounds are open from 10 a.m. to 6.30 p.m., and a shuttle bus will carry you along the 4km of tarmac to the base of Ben Crom Dam (the bus operates daily in July and August, and on weekends only during May, June and September).

At other times of the year, consider accessing the route from the north, starting and finishing at the Trassey Track car park. Follow the Trassey Track south to Hare's Gap, then follow the route described from there. This variation adds an extra 6km and 280m ascent to the day.

The Walk

From the end of the road beneath Ben Crom Reservoir, begin by climbing the steps on the right-hand side of the dam. Cross the fence around the reservoir and climb northeast, crossing the steep lower slopes of Slieve Binnian on your way to the boggy col between Binnian and Slievelamagan.

At the col, join a faint footpath leading northeast up the boulder-strewn slopes of Slievelamagan. The ascent is steady with little respite in the gradient. The view from the top is as good as you would expect from the most central peak in the Mournes. Especially memorable is the view to the northwest, where Slieve Bearnagh looms over the dark waters of Ben Crom.

The Mourne Mountains from the summit of Slieve Bearnagh.

Follow the path north from the summit. Descend across a col before climbing slightly across the uninspiring hump of Cove Mountain. Another short descent is followed by a choice of either contouring around the western slopes of Slieve Beg or climbing straight over the top to reach the well-worn path of the Brandy Pad, an old smuggler's trail through the mountains.

Turn left and follow the Brandy Pad west towards the conspicuous green notch of Hare's Gap. Around halfway along, the path rounds a small gully and passes behind a curious pillar-like boulder. You are now at the very head of the Silent Valley and there are tremendous views into the deep basin below. Continue to Hare's Gap, where you meet the Mourne Wall. This is another water-related construction, built between 1910 and 1922 to encircle the watershed of the Silent and Annalong Valleys.

Turn left in front of the wall and climb southwest up a flight of steps. There is little respite in the ascent until you arrive at the north tor of Slieve Bearnagh. Follow a path around the southern side of this outcrop, then rejoin the Mourne Wall in the col between Bearnagh's twin tops. A short climb now brings you to the huge summit tor. On a good day you will have little trouble appreciating why this one of the best-loved peaks in the Mournes.

Follow the southern side of the wall as it zigzags on top of Bearnagh, then plunges steeply west to the col between Bearnagh and Slieve Meelmore. At the col, join a rough path that heads southwest around the base of Slieve Meelmore and Slieve Meelbeg. Follow the path past Blue Lough, then head south across broken ground towards Ben Crom River. Pick up a faint path beside the river and follow it southeast. When the path peters out, keep contouring across the slopes of Ben Crom to reach a point overlooking a footbridge on the Mill River.

Descend steeply to the bridge, cross the river, and you will arrive back at the road beneath Ben Crom dam.

ROUTE 10:
The Binnians

An excellent circuit over two distinctive summits, offering some sustained, high-level walking.

Grade:	4
Time:	4½–5½ hours
Distance:	13km (8 miles)
Ascent:	625m (1,900ft)
Map:	OSNI 1:50,000 sheet 29, or OSNI 1:25,000 *The Mournes.*

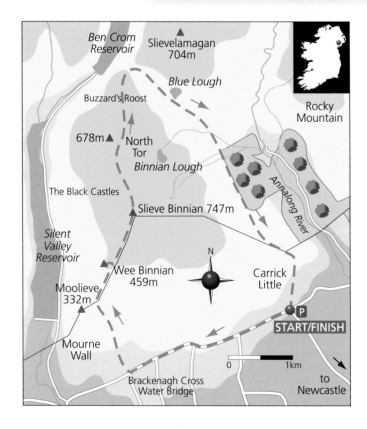

Start & Finish: The route starts and finishes at Carrick Little car park, roughly 4km west of Annalong village (grid reference: J345219). Annalong village is situated on the A2, 9km north of Kilkeel and 11km south of Newcastle. In the centre of Annalong, turn northwest opposite a church and begin up Majors Hill Road. Around 2km later, turn right onto Oldtown Road. Carrick Little car park is situated just past a T-Junction some 2km later.

At the southeastern corner of the Mourne Mountains, two summits stand together like big brother and little brother. Thanks to their location, Slieve Binnian (747m) and Wee Binnian (459m) provide fantastic views over both the rugged heartland of the Mournes and the pastoral coastline to the south.

Yet the most distinctive feature of these mountains is not their views, but the granite tors that crown their summits, ranking them amongst the most interesting peaks in Ireland. The tors were sculpted during the last ice age, when the summits protruded above the glaciers as nunataks. Exposure to severe frost weathering meant that soil and weaker layers of granite were eroded away to leave these fascinating formations.

Though it is a fairly short circuit by some standards, the steep ascent makes it feel quite strenuous. Informal paths have formed over much of the route, but you will need good navigation skills in bad weather. The route begins with 2.5km of road walking. If you have two vehicles this tarmac section can be avoided by leaving a second car near Brackenagh Cross Water Bridge, 2.5km west of the start.

The view along the Mourne Wall from Slieve Binnian to Wee Binnian.

The Walk

From Carrick Little car park, join the road and walk west along the tarmac for 2.5km to Brackenagh Cross Water Bridge. Cross the bridge and 50m later, look for a track that leads north off the road. Turn right and head up the track, climbing steadily towards the col between Moolieve and Wee Binnian. After 500m the track breaks up into several rougher trails. Keep straight ahead, heading directly towards the col.

Just beneath the col you reach the Mourne Wall and a heavy iron gate. At this point you have a choice of routes. For the adventurous option, stay on the southern side of the wall and follow it northwest. As you round the side of the mountain you come to a deep gully that cuts the main tor in two. Climb through the gully, making a strenuous heave over a rock step halfway up. Several rock climbs start from here, and the scramble up the gully itself was given a climbing grade in the Victorian era.

For the easier option, go through the gate and follow the northern side of the wall towards Wee Binnian. Where the wall ends at the foot of the summit tor, follow a path around the northern slopes of the mountain.

Whichever way you reach Wee Binnian, you must now descend northeast to a col. The shoulder of Slieve Binnian now rises ahead of you in a single, relentless sweep of more than 300m. The Mourne Wall runs directly up the shoulder, and you should climb steeply along the southern side of this, enjoying increasingly extensive views as you gain height.

The wall peters out a short distance beneath the summit at the foot of some steep rock slabs. Climb to the right of the slabs and head up into a gap between two subsidiary tors. Exit the gap at the eastern side of the mountain and join a well-defined path around the base of the summit tor.

From the summit the path heads north across a broad shoulder, descending gently towards several smaller tors on the otherwise flat terrain. These are known as the Black Castles, and the path skirts across the rocky base of the largest outcrop. The view across the Mournes is superb from here, encompassing virtually every peak in the range.

Beyond the Black Castles the path descends to a broad col. The North Tor is now 400m away to the northeast, and the path suggests that most people skip point 678m and contour directly to this landmark. Head around the western side of North Tor and begin the main descent. Keep to the shoulder of Binnian's north ridge, which becomes narrower as you near the col beneath Slievelamagan.

Once in the col, join a path that descends southeast past Blue Lough. The path becomes a track above Annalong Wood, then turns into a laneway. Continue straight ahead at all junctions to arrive back at Carrick Little car park.

Slieve Foye

The highest summit in County Louth provides great views, and is easily accessible from the historic village of Carlingford.

Grade:	4
Time:	4–5 hours
Distance:	11.5km (7 miles)
Ascent:	730m (2,400ft)
Map:	OSNI 1:50,000 sheet 29

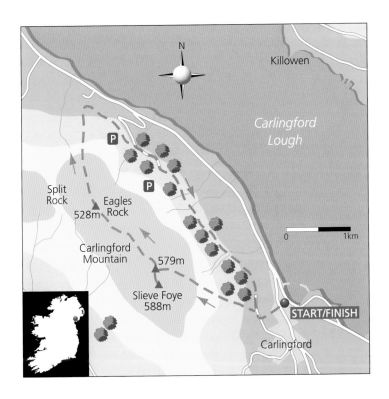

Climbing Slieve Foye above the village of Carlingford.

Start & Finish: The route starts and finishes at the tourist office car park in the village of Carlingford, on the northern side of the Cooley Peninsula (grid reference: J189116). The tourist office is located along the waterfront, at back of the harbour.

At 588m high, Slieve Foye is the highest peak in the Cooley Mountains of County Louth. Rising steeply above the castle ruins and pretty streets of the medieval fishing village of Carlingford, the rocky outcrops along its upper ridge and the fabulous summit views make this a popular mountain. The waymarked Táin Way also traverses the lower slopes, providing an easy return section along forest tracks.

Access is straightforward, with the novelty of starting and finishing right in the heart of the village. Descending off the hill and heading straight into one of Carlingford's pubs, cafés or bistros really adds to the atmosphere of the day. A word of caution for the inexperienced: Slieve Foye is hardly a giant, but there is some rough and potentially dangerous ground that can cause confusion in poor visibility. The unusual magnetic properties of the gabbro rock can also interfere with compasses, so care is required with navigation.

The Walk

Three signed loop walks start at the tourist office car park, and they all follow the same initial route as our circuit. This means you can begin by following the blue, green and red arrows through the village. From the car park entrance, turn left and walk along the road past sixteenth-century Taaffe's Castle. Turn left then right at the next two junctions to reach the centre of the village. Keep straight ahead here, climbing past a prominent collection of signposts and onto a narrow lane.

At the top of the road, turn right, still following the blue and red arrows. Follow a track for 300m to the edge of a forest plantation. You will return along the track at the end of the route, but for now, turn left and cross a stile, joining a path that climbs steeply along the southern edge of the forest. Where the plantation ends, continue straight ahead across steep, open slopes, heading northwest along the course of a small stream.

The gradient eases as you arrive at a small basin beneath the intimidating gabbro crags that guard this side of the summit. Pass around the side of the outcrop, then bear northwest and climb into a wide gully. This brings you to a grassy col, where you should turn abruptly south. Informal paths appear underfoot as you wind between rock outcrops to arrive at the summit cairn and trig point at the top of Slieve Foye. The views are fabulous, both northeast across Carlingford Lough to the Mourne Mountains, and southeast across Dundalk Bay and the Isle of Man.

Turn around now and retrace your steps north. Descend back to the col, then head northwest towards a prominent slab of gabbro marked on the map as point 579m. An easy scramble across rough rock brings you to the top, though you can just as easily bypass the outcrop on the left.

A short, steep descent leads onto the middle section of the summit ridge, where the ground becomes softer underfoot. Here the route veers west and drops across a small rise. A more pronounced descent then takes you past a steep, overhanging crag on the left, and brings you to a wide col beneath Eagles Rock.

Make the short climb to the flat, rocky summit of Eagles Rock (528m). At this stage there is an optional detour to Ravens Rock and Foxes Rock, which will add 1½ to 2 hours to your day. However, the main route descends north across increasingly rough ground, heading towards the northwestern tip of Slieve Foye Forest. The trees have been cleared here, but you should be able to make out the boundary fence that surrounds the plantation.

At the northwestern corner of the fence, continue north and descend for 20m with the fence on your right. Here you join the signed route of the Táin Way; turn right and cross a stile over the fence. Join the end of a forest track that passes though alternating patches of mature and clear-felled trees. After 1km, descend to a larger track and keep straight ahead, following the marker posts southeast for a further 3km. You rejoin your outward route just above Carlingford. Turn left onto the road and descend the short distance to the coffee houses below.

Melmore Head

With majestic Boyeeghter Strand as its centrepiece, the circuit of remote Melmore Head is one of Donegal's finest coastal walks.

Grade:	4
Time:	4–5 hours
Distance:	12.5km (8 miles)
Ascent:	200m (660ft)
Map:	OSi 1:50,000 sheet 2

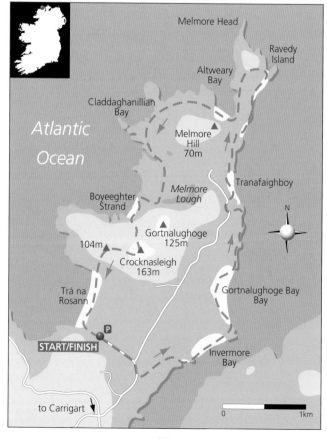

Start & Finish: The route starts and finishes at Trá na Rosann car park, on the western side of Melmore Head (grid reference: C118420). Begin by following the R245 to the village of Carrickart. As you leave Carrickart, turn right onto the R248, signed for Downings. Roughly 2km later, continue straight ahead at a junction, onto a minor road signed to Melmore Head. Follow this for 6km, until it descends onto a flat expanse of machair. Turn left at a sign for Trá na Rosann, and continue to the large car park at the end of the road.

M elmore Head lies at the northwest tip of the Rosguill peninsula. The eastern shore of the headland is low and softened by a succession of sandy beaches, while the west coast is wilder, punctuated by deep inlets and rugged hills. The beaches range from sweeping strands to tiny coves, and amongst it all lies Boyeeghter Strand, one of the most dramatic beaches in Ireland.

The route begins with 1.5km of road walking, but continues across beaches, dunes and grassy hills. The exact route may depend on the tide: at low water you can walk across firm sand, while high tide may force you onto the land above. The toughest section is kept to the end – a steep ascent to the 163m summit of Crocknasleigh – though the views more than justify the effort.

The Walk

Begin by walking back along the road to the car park. Turn right at the main road, then turn left 200m later. Follow this lane for 500m to the end of the road. Now continue straight ahead onto a grassy footpath, descending through two pedestrian gates to reach the sandy cove of Inverbeg Bay.

Turn left here and begin to follow the coastline north. After Inverbeg Bay, pass over a low headland to reach Invermore Bay. Another grassy promontory gives access to the beautiful, curving beach at Gortnalughoge Bay. At the northern end of Gortnalughoge, the route depends on the tide: at high tide, follow a path through the dunes, just above the coast; at low tide, continue along the shore, passing three small coves before climbing to the path above. Follow the trail over a wooden stile before reaching a place where the coastal route is barred by a deep inlet and a tall metal fence. Turn left here and follow the fence inland for 100m to reach a road.

Turn right along the tarmac for 150m, then return to the shoreline at Tranafaighaboy beach. At the northern end of this beach, head left between two mobile homes, then turn right onto a track. Pass a vehicle barrier and follow the track through the caravans for 200m to reach the narrow neck of dune that connects Melmore Head to the mainland.

At low tide, drop east onto a beach, then follow the shoreline north towards the small lighthouse on Ravedy Island. Here you can descend a flight of steps and visit the rocky islet itself. At high tide, follow the track until it swings left, then continue straight ahead on a grassy path. At a path junction, turn right and climb over a stile beside a gate. You can now begin an anticlockwise circuit around the headland towards Ravedy Island.

From Ravedy Island, climb west to reach the remains of an old signal tower at the 58m summit of Melmore Head. The coastal views are extensive, encompassing Fanad Head and Malin Head to the east, and the 200m-high cliffs of Horn Head to the west. Descend south along the headland's west coast. Cross the stile to arrive at the cliff-backed beach in Altweary Bay. If the tide is low you can walk cross the beach and scramble up the rocks at its western end. At high tide you may have to climb over Melmore Hill (70m), then descend northwest to rejoin the coastal route.

The next stretch of coastline is flat and rocky with a conspicuous grassy headland. Pass a storm beach and small enclosure before turning south past Claddaghanillian Bay. The route now veers inland to circumvent a long, narrow inlet. Head south from the end of the inlet to reach Melmore Lough.

From the western end of the lough, follow a high stone wall across a short rise, where a gap in the wall lets you cross onto a promontory. Below lies Boyeeghter Strand, surely one of the wildest and most beautiful beaches in Ireland. At high tide or in stormy weather you may not be able to reach the main strand, and will have to climb south across the hill above the beach. At other times, cross back through the wall and head north for 100m, where you can descend through the dunes to the sand. If conditions are right, be sure to visit the cave at the back of the main beach.

Leave the beach via a steep grassy gully at its southern end. Continue climbing the steep slope above to reach a superlative viewpoint atop Crocknasleigh, some 163m above the sea. The climb is strenuous, but the remarkable views from the top provide a fitting finale. To descend back to the start, head west towards point 104m, then drop south onto Trá na Rosann. Cross to the southern end of the beach, then head left along a sandy path and wooden boardwalk that returns you to the car park.

View over Boyeeghter Strand and Melmore Head from Crocknasleigh.

Muckish

Follow a historic trail up precipitous rock buttresses to reach the top of this distinctive, flat–topped mountain.

Grade:	4
Time:	2–3 hours
Distance:	4.5km (3 miles)
Ascent:	400m (1,310ft)
Map:	OSi 1:50,000 sheet 2

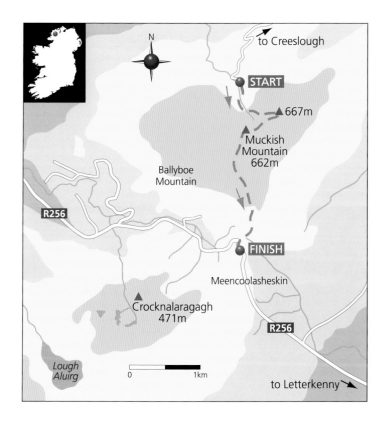

Start & Finish: The route starts on the northern side of Muckish (grid reference: C998294). Begin by following the N56 to Creeslough. Around 2km north of this village, turn west onto the L1282 to Derryharriff. Pass a stone works, then keep left over a cattle grid. Climb past signs for various loop walks and park in a stony clearing about 80m before the end the tarmac.

The route finishes at Muckish Gap (grid reference: B998268). This is located along a minor road between Falcarragh and the R251. Park beside a shrine on the northern side of the gap, where there is space for at least four cars.

The distinctive tabletop profile of 667m-high Muckish is as much an icon of north Donegal as its neighbour Errigal. From the top, impressive summit views encompass much of the north Donegal coastline as well as the Derryveagh Mountains. The mountain's towering cliffs consist of sandstone mixed with deposits of concentrated quartzite. The sand form of this quartzite is unusually pure, and until its closure in 1955, a mine extracted this sand for use in the manufacture of high-quality optical glass.

For walkers, there are two main routes to the summit. The Miners' Track is a historic access route that miners once used to reach their quarry high on the northern cliffs of the mountain. Another route approaches from Muckish Gap to the south. The walk described here follows both routes as it makes a full traverse of the peak. The trailheads are a long way apart by road, however, and you will need two vehicles to make the route possible. Alternatively, consider an out-and-back trip from one end or the other.

Heading southwest along the barren summit plateau of Muckish.

Of the two routes, the Miners' Track is more interesting historically and topographically, but the ground is steeper, rockier and more exposed than the approach from Muckish Gap.

Whichever route you chose, make sure to take care with the weather. On a clear day it is a simple task to navigate around the plateau, but in bad visibility solid navigational skills are required to avoid getting lost amid the featureless terrain.

The Walk

From the parking area, walk to the end of the road, then continue along a rough vehicle track to the concrete loading bays at the bottom of the old mine. The area is littered with the first of many pieces of discarded machinery, rusty reminders of a bygone industry.

Join the path beneath the right-hand concrete block, then cross a stream and begin the steep ascent. Though once carefully maintained, the trail has now fallen into disrepair and caution must be exercised in places. The route ahead is generally obvious, with low stone walls crossing any side-trails. From below it is just possible to make out a procession of stakes clinging to the rock buttresses above, marking the line of ascent.

Start by picking your way beside, then along, a rubble spur to the right of the stream. The point where the spur meets the rock face is marked by a pole. The route from here is exposed and not for the faint-hearted. In some places steps have been cut into the rock, while in others you have to pick your way carefully over loose stones. At a fork about two thirds of the way up, keep right and use your hands to mount a high rock step. White sand becomes more abundant until you reach the hollowed basin of the quarry itself, with old machinery still perched precariously in front of the Atlantic backdrop.

Now drop back down the path a couple of steps and traverse left under the lip of the quarry. Swing back right and negotiate the last piece of exposed ground before making a sudden exit onto the wide, rock-strewn plateau. Head northeast to reach the summit cairn and trig point, which boasts fantastic coastal views. Then cross the plateau to reach a second cairn around 600m southwest. From here the vista is dominated by the noble cone of Errigal, backed by the other peaks of the Derryveagh Mountains.

From the southern cairn, follow the eastern edge of the plateau as it curves around to the left. Precipitous scree slopes make descent impossible further west. Drop off the plateau at its southeastern tip and join a peat track. The descent is steep, but heathery slopes contrast sharply with the rock buttresses of the Miners' Track. Make for the nearest point of the road and turn left onto the tarmac. The shrine that marks Muckish Gap is just a minute's walk away.

ROUTE 14:
Errigal

Known as the Monarch of the Northwest, Errigal is one of the most
distinctive and exciting summits in Ireland.

Southeast Ridge	
Grade:	4
Time:	2½–3 hours
Distance:	5km (3 miles)
Ascent:	510m (1,670ft)
Map:	OSi 1:50,000 sheet 1

Northeast Ridge	
Grade:	5
Time:	2½–3 hours
Distance:	5km (3 miles)
Ascent:	510m (1,670ft)
Map:	OSi 1:50,000 sheet 1

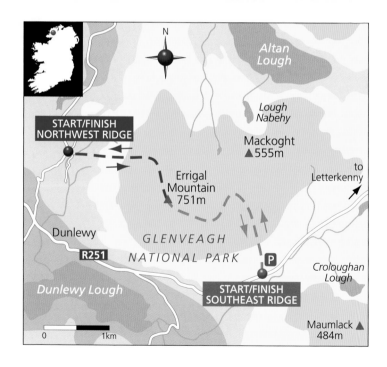

Errigal Mountain, in the far northwest of Donegal, is one of Ireland's natural icons. A distinctive and exciting peak, it boasts incredible views from its 751m-high summit. The mountain is readily accessible and easily navigated, and attracts large numbers of walkers, the vast majority of whom ascend the peak via the 'tourist route' of the southeast ridge. The volume of feet has caused problems with erosion over the years and work continues to try to alleviate wear at the bottom of this path.

Despite the popularity of the southeast ridge, the route should not be dismissed as easy or dull; the exposure of the summit ridge will keep even the most experienced walker entertained. The other main route on the mountain is the far less frequented and more challenging northwest ridge, which involves a small amount of scrambling. We describe both approach routes here, although with two vehicles or a bike you can enjoy the best possible option and combine the two in a full traverse of the mountain.

In high winds, great care is required to venture onto Errigal's summit ridge. Walkers who want to extend the route can also add an ascent of 555m-high Mackoght, just northeast of Errigal.

The Southeast Ridge

Start & Finish: This route starts and finishes at a walled car park on the northern side of the R251, around 4.5km east of Dunlewy (grid reference: B943197).

From the car park, follow well-spaced marker posts north along the course of a stream. The ground can be very wet in places and you should be wary of patches of treacherous green moss. The posts lead you to the rugged col between Errigal and Mackoght, with its curious outcrops of quartzite. From here you can see the full extent of the southeast ridge arcing across the sky, with the mountain's north face falling almost vertically beneath it.

The path that winds southwest up Errigal's lower slopes is also clearly visible. Join this rough, gravel-strewn trail and climb steeply until the ridge begins to narrow. At this point the path flattens out a little and rounds a rock outcrop, bringing you to a broad, level area with a stone shelter and cairn that acts as a memorial to local mountaineer Joey Glover.

The ridge narrows to a knife-edge just beneath the top. The sensational summit is one of the smallest in Ireland, with room for no more than a couple of people to stand at any one time. The second, slightly lower summit lies roughly 50m away across a notch. On a clear day the views are panoramic, extending over much of Ulster and as far south as the cliffs of Mayo. For the descent, simply reverse your outward journey.

Walking along Errigal's airy summit ridge.

The Northwest Ridge

Start & Finish: This route starts and finishes in a small lay-by at the start of a bog track at grid reference: B914215. Head to the village of Dunlewy and locate a pub on the northern side of the road. Turn north on the left side of this building and follow the lane for 1.5km to a junction with the bog track.

From the lay-by, follow the old bog track up to a flat area of peat hags and old turf cuttings. Cross this, heading towards the northwestern base of the mountain. There are two steep ascents to negotiate before you reach the ridge itself. Keep to the left on both climbs, following a shallow gully up the first slope, and enjoying a slightly milder gradient on the second.

Now follow a small ridge around the north of a scree-filled hollow, to arrive at the base of the northwest ridge. You are now faced with a 30° scree slope; a challenge akin to climbing a sand dune in terms of return for energy expended. Yet there is no other option except to attack the ridge directly and try not to slide back too much.

Conditions improve underfoot after 200m of altitude, and several rock outcrops should be passed on the right. The ridge begins to narrow now; confident scramblers will keep to the crest as much as possible, though the difficulties can always be avoided on the right. Beware of slipping on loose rock, and take care not to dislodge stones onto climbers below.

There is a brief, flat section before another band of rock outcrops brings you to the narrow summit ridge. Errigal's secondary summit is now just a short distance away, with the main summit 50m south across a shallow col. For the descent you can either retrace your steps, or return down the southeastern ridge and back along the road through Dunlewy.

Slieve Snaght and the Poisoned Glen

This wild and rewarding walk explores the brooding confines of the Poisoned Glen and the rocky peaks above.

Grade:	4
Time:	5½–6½ hours
Distance:	14km (9 miles)
Ascent:	870m (2,850ft)
Map:	OSi 1:50,000 sheet 1

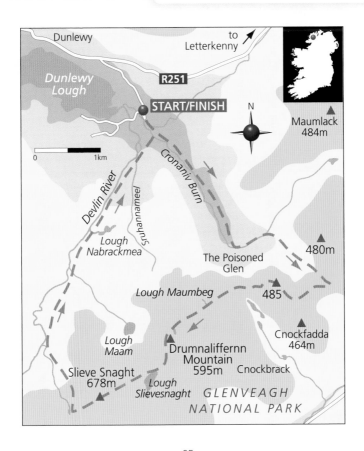

Twisted tree and stream at the base of the Poisoned Glen.

Start & Finish: The route starts and finishes at the bottom of a track at grid reference: B930189. Begin by heading along the R251 to Dunlewy. Around 1km east of the village, turn south onto a minor road signed to the Poisoned Glen. Pass a roofless church and park beside a hairpin bend with a track leading off to the left. There is room here for four cars, and further space beside the roofless church.

The wild granite dome of Slieve Snaght lies at the heart of a lonely landscape of lochs, bogs and ice-carved cliffs that make up the greater part of Glenveagh National Park. Beneath these rocky, lake-studded uplands is the Poisoned Glen, a wild, brooding valley hemmed in on three sides by 300m-high cliffs. One story recounts how the glen was named after the poisonous Irish Spurge that grew along the banks of the Cronaniv Burn, while another maintains that no bird ever flies in the valley. Either way this is an atmospheric and challenging route, and you will feel a great sense of achievement after completing it.

Try to avoid walking in poor visibility to avoid the navigational difficulties between Ballaghgeeha Gap and Slieve Snaght. It is also worth waiting for a dry spell or a hard winter freeze because the Derryveagh Mountains drain poorly, and the floor of the Poisoned Glen can be little short of a quagmire after a period of rain.

The Walk

From the hairpin bend, follow the track southeast towards the Poisoned Glen. The track crosses a beautiful old stone bridge across a tributary of the Cronaniv Burn, then loses itself in the dampness of the valley floor.

The terrain here can be very wet after rain, though the conditions improve towards the head of the glen.

Continue to follow the eastern bank of the river into the glen. As you pick up a more distinct track, the walls and crags begin to close in on either side. Ahead lies the imposing buttress known as the Castle. Before you reach the foot of this crag, veer left and climb along a stream.

You must now make your first crossing of the national park's deer fence, a 45km-long enclosure that contains the largest herd of deer in Ireland. Veer right, away from the stream, to pass through a metal gate in the fence. Now cross a flat valley, heading towards the boulder-filled gully at its head. Climb steeply into the gully, following a grassy path between the rocks to arrive at the notched col known as the Ballaghgeeha Gap.

In poor visibility, this is where navigational problems begin. Even in clear weather, route finding is not always straightforward. The rugged landscape is typical of the Derryveagh range, with granite outcrops and glacial erratics punctuating a sea of bog, heather and small lochans. Overall, it is all quite wild and beautiful.

From Ballaghgeeha Gap, climb west to point 454m. Now descend southwest to a shallow col, before veering northwest to reach the small cairn that marks point 485m. On the way you will have to recross the deer fence, which is most easily achieved by squeezing between the wire. Now descend west to the col above Lough Atirrive Big, where precipitous cliffs allow a bird's-eye view into the Poisoned Glen below.

From the col, climb west towards Drumnaliffernn Mountain, a confusing hump of broken, undulating ground. Head southwest from the southern shore of Lough Maumbeg to reach the summit cairn. Now continue southwest, past another small lough, to reach the top of steep cliffs. Follow the cliff edge south into the rocky col just east of Lough Slievesnaght, where there is a fine view across the lake to the looming hulk of Slieve Snaght itself.

Descend around the northern shore of Lough Slievesnaght, then begin a steady ascent of 200 vertical metres to the cairn that marks the broad summit. The panorama includes a winning combination of mountain and coastline, with the distinctive cone of Errigal dominant to the north.

To descend most easily, head southwest from the summit then drop down towards Loch an Ghainimh, keeping the steeper slopes on your right. From the lake, descend north. A band of large boulders forms a brief obstacle before you can turn northwest and contour across easier ground to join the Devlin River just north of a prominent waterfall.

All that is left now is to follow the southern bank of the beautiful Devlin River downstream, with Errigal a constant presence ahead. Close to the finish, cross the Sruhannameel stream then head east across Cronaniv Burn. Turn left onto the track you used at the start of the circuit and retrace your initial steps to the finish.

Glenveagh and Farscallop

A scenic track along a glacial valley leads to a short but demanding hill-walk with fine views.

Grade:	4
Time:	4½–5½ hours
Distance:	15.5km (9½ miles)
Ascent:	440m (1,440ft)
Map:	OSi 1:50,000 sheet 6

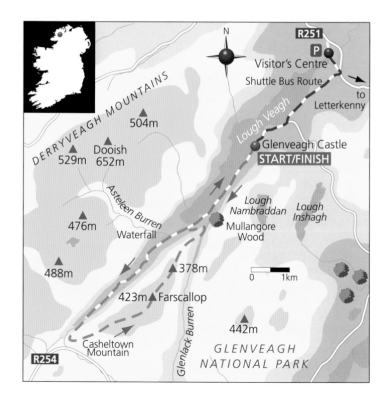

Start & Finish: This route starts and finishes at Glenveagh Castle (grid reference: C021210). Begin by heading to Glenveagh National Park, which is well signed along the R251. Entry to the large car park and adjacent visitor centre is free, but there is a €3 charge for the shuttle bus, which carries you along 3km of road to and from Glenveagh Castle.

Alternatively, you could start at the park's rear entrance at Casheltown Mountain (grid reference: B971158). Consult the OS map to navigate your way to this point. The entrance lies at the apex of a bend, where a conspicuous track leads off to the northeast. Parking is limited to just two cars.

Glenveagh National Park is one of the Irish state's finest acquisitions, purchased from the McIlhenny family in 1975. Subsequent purchases of adjoining land have swelled the park to some 170 square kilometres, and guaranteed walking access to the rugged heart of the Derryveagh Mountains.

This route explores a wide diversity of terrain. Beginning at nineteenth-century Glenveagh Castle on the shore of beautiful Lough Veagh, it follows a firm, low-level track to the head of a glacial valley. Here it leaves the path and embarks on a trip across 423m Farscallop, crossing open mountain terrain and enjoying good views across the similarly rugged landscape of the surrounding peaks. A descent through an ancient oak wood completes the circuit. As you walk, keep your eyes open for red deer – the park contains the largest herd in Ireland – and for golden eagles, which were reintroduced here in 2001.

The ground on the southern slopes of Farscallop can be wet and boggy, so it is worth keeping the route for a dry spell or hard winter freeze.

Pool near the summit of Farscallop, with Lough Veagh behind.

The park is open from 9 a.m. to 5 p.m. during the winter, and until 6 p.m. in the summer. Note that mountain access may be restricted between August and February during the deer cull. To check access before you walk, contact the ranger on tel: 076 1002 548.

The Walk

From the car park and visitor centre, begin by taking the shuttle bus to nineteenth-century Glenveagh Castle. Walk around the southern side of this building and begin to follow a track southwest along the shores of Lough Veagh. In less than 1km you reach eaves of Mullangore Wood, a valuable remnant of ancient oakwood. Continue past the beach at the end of Lough Veagh, then keep straight ahead at a junction with a smaller track that comes down from Glenlack to your left (you will return along this track later).

The trees begin to dissipate as you pass an old stalker's cottage and a walled garden. Climb gradually along the track into the wilder upper reaches of the glen. The Owenveagh River now runs immediately to your right, and views open up across the valley to Astelleen Waterfall, which descends some 200m in a series of impressive cascades. The gradient increases as you climb towards the head of the valley, and you reach a gate in the deer fence roughly two hours from Glenveagh Castle. The R254 lies just beyond this gate.

Stay inside the fence and turn left, climbing east and then northeast along the broad shoulder of Farscallop. The ground here can be rather wet underfoot. As you cross the 350m contour, the heather and grass are replaced by peat hags and you will have weave your way through the maze. Fortunately the difficulties are short-lived and conditions improve as you reach Farscallop's summit cairn. Fine views now include Errigal and the Derryveagh Mountains to the northwest, and the Gartan Valley to the south.

Descend northeast from Farscallop, keeping an eye open for red deer, which favour this part of the park. The first half of the descent is relatively easy, with fabulous views across Lough Veagh. Cross the rise at 378m and continue northeast along the crest of the ridge. The slope soon begins to fall away more steeply, and you will have to pick your way through some rugged granite outcrops. Head for the point where the spur meets Mullangore Wood. In clear conditions the line of descent is obvious, pointing you directly towards the distant turrets of Glenveagh Castle.

Once in the wood you quickly join the track coming down from Glenlack. In spring the banks of this track are covered by primroses and wood anemone. Turn left and descend back to the shore of Lough Veagh, then turn right onto the main track to return to Glenveagh Castle.

Glencolmcille Circuit

The combination of ancient monuments and striking coastline makes this a memorable outing for any walker.

Grade:	3
Time:	4–5 hours
Distance:	13km (8 miles)
Ascent:	500m (1,640ft)
Map:	OSi 1:50,000 sheet 10

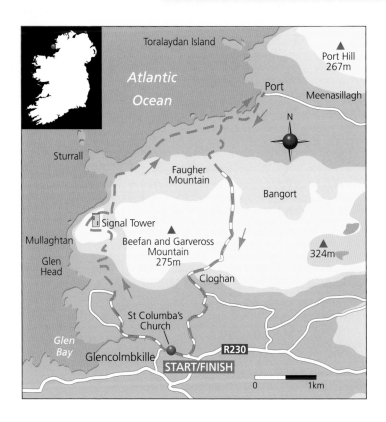

Start & Finish: The route starts and finishes at St Columba's Church in the centre of Glencolmcille (grid reference: G535849). Glencolmcille is located around 24km west of Killybegs along the R263. A small car park in front of the church provides space for around ten vehicles.

Glencolmcille is a remote and atmospheric village steeped in history. Human settlement dates back 5,000 years and the village is surrounded by a remarkable number of Neolithic and Early Christian monuments. In many cases, former pagan sites have been given new meaning within the Christian faith, and thousands of pilgrims still visit the area each year to pray at the fifteen ancient stations of the Turas.

The village is also surrounded by some of the wildest and most spectacular coastline in the country. Well-informed hillwalkers have long been making the journey from here to the deserted village of Port, but the development of several signed walking routes simplifies both access and route finding. The route described here is a 'mix and match' circuit that uses the Tower Loop, Drum Loop and Bealach na Gaeltachta – all of which are signed – as well as crossing as a stretch of open coastline. The terrain underfoot is a mixture of laneway, track and open hillside.

Though roughly two thirds of the route is waymarked in some form, a map and navigation skills are still required for the open section. Care is also required along the top of exposed cliffs.

The Walk

The first part of the route follows the blue arrows of the Tower Loop. From St Columba's Church, head west along the road. After just 80m you reach the day's first antiquity: an Early Christian carved pillar set on the right side of the road, with access via a small flight of stone steps.

Turn right at the next junction and pass the sandbars of the Murlin River estuary. Cross a bridge then turn right again to pass Turas Station No. 3 – a small Mass rock beside a cairn. Veer right in front of a cottage and climb along a grassy boreen to a junction. Turn left here for 80m, then pass through a gate on the right and begin to climb along a rocky track. Signs indicate Columcille's Well off to the right here, which consists of a court cairn and adjacent holy well set in a hollow.

The track heads up the open hillside, with increasing views across Skelpoonagh Bay. Climb through several switchbacks to a fork near the top of the hill. Turn left here and continue across a gentle, peaty slope to reach a prominent signal tower at the top of Glen Head. This imposing structure is one of several Napoleonic towers that grace the headlands around Glencolmcille. The cliffs beneath the building are some 200m high, and there is a fabulous coastal panorama in both directions.

Looking towards the promontory of Sturrall, just north of the signal tower.

Leave the signed loop walk here and begin to head northeast along the coast, following an informal path through the grass. A short distance beyond the signal tower, the dramatic arête of Sturrall thrusts into the sea, its white rock, curving spine and precipitous sides making it one of the most distinctive coastal formations in Ireland.

Continue to follow the coast northeast, taking care near the clifftop. Descend across a hollow, then veer east, heading diagonally inland across a kilometre of rough, heather-covered ground. The view ahead is dominated by the huge cliffs beneath Port Hill and the jumble of massive sea stacks in the bay below. When you meet a bog track signed as part of the Bealach na Gaeltachta, turn left and make the final descent to Port. This village was deserted in the 1940s, and the ruined stone buildings combine with the awesome scenery to make it an extremely evocative place. You will be forgiven for lingering a while to explore further.

When you are ready, return to the track you used on your outward journey. Climb steadily for some 260 vertical metres to reach a communication mast on the barren summit of Beefan and Garveross Mountain. Cross straight over a junction at the top of the hill, then descend steeply along a lane, soon rejoining the route marked by the blue arrows.

Near the bottom of the slope you pass *Mainnear na Mortlaidh*, a court tomb believed to date from 3000 BC. A short distance further along the road is *Cloch Aonach* (the Meeting Stone), a carved pillar with a hole near the top that was used during pagan marriage rituals. At the end of the road, turn right to return to the church where the route began.

ROUTE 18:
Slieve League Traverse

The route over Donegal's most majestic sea cliffs is a classic of the region, with a full traverse the most fulfilling option available.

Grade:	4
Time:	4½–5½ hours
Distance:	15km (9½ miles)
Ascent:	570m (1,870ft)
Map:	OSi 1:50,000 sheet 10

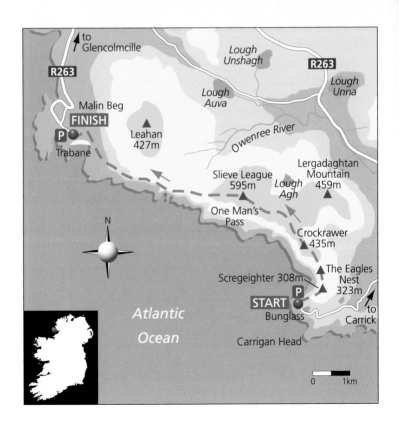

View across the mighty cliffs of Slieve League from Bunglas.

Start & Finish: The route starts at Bunglass car park (grid reference: G558757). To reach this point, head through Carrick and Teelin, then turn right along a steep road signed for Bunglass. Pass though a gate (be careful to close it behind you) and continue to the parking area at the end of the road.

The route finishes at a car park at the end of the road in Malin Beg (grid reference: G498800.

With the possible exception of Errigal, the trip to the summit of Slieve League is the most popular hill-walk in northwest Ireland. Viewed from inland, it is an unremarkable whaleback of a mountain. Move to the seaward side however, and you cannot help but be awestruck by the scale of the cliffs that plunge dramatically into the Atlantic. Thousands of years of wave action have eaten away at the mountain's southwestern face, leaving sheer rock faces and precipitous slopes that stretch for 2km at over 500m high. Only Croaghaun on Achill Island can compete in terms of grandeur in Ireland.

By far the best route on the mountain is the full traverse from Bunglass to Malin Beg. However, you will need to arrange return transport to complete this linear walk, using either a second vehicle or a local taxi firm. Otherwise, consider an out-and-back trip from Bunglass. The alternative Pilgrims' Path, which climbs the mountain from Teelin to the southeast, is rather mundane in comparison with the coastal routes.

Much of the walk is spent alongside sheer drops. Avoid walking in poor visibility or strong winds, and take the utmost care near the edge.

The Walk

The route starts with a bang straight from Bunglass car park. If you have never been here before, the sudden sight of the cliffs falling half a kilometre into the ocean is utterly absorbing. Begin by taking a well-constructed, flagstone path that leaves from the northeastern corner of the car park. The trail is maintained for the first section, where the number of passing feet is greatest.

Head northeast around the cliffs, climbing several flights of steps to reach Scregeighter (308m). The path now becomes more informal, though it remains obvious underfoot. Swing northwest and climb along the cliff edge to The Eagles Nest (323m), where the drop to the ocean is almost vertical.

The path now moves away from the cliffs and crosses a couple of small rises. Climb diagonally across the heather-covered slopes to reach Crockrawer at 435m. Descend briefly to a col, then begin a scenic climb along the top of an obvious ridge. At one point the apex of this ridge narrows to an exposed rib of rock, half a metre wide and around 15m long, with dangerous drops on both sides. Although the OS map marks One Man's Pass higher up the mountain, many Irish walkers believe the label has been misplaced, and this section is certainly more deserving of the name. In dry, calm conditions the section can be negotiated with a straightforward scramble, though you will need to have a good head for heights. Otherwise, take the easy alternative path on the right, which skirts around the base of the crag and rejoins the crest of the ridge a little higher up.

The ridge broadens now and you soon emerge onto Slieve League's peat-covered eastern summit (560m). The true summit lies a kilometre further northwest, across another fine ridge (this is the section that has been wrongly marked on the OS map as One Man's Pass). This ridge is enjoyably airy, but can be crossed without breaking stride. The official high point of 595m Slieve League is marked by a trig pillar and fabulous views in all directions. On a clear day, Errigal, Benbulbin and even Croagh Patrick can all be identified on the horizon.

If you are continuing to Malin Beg, head west from the summit and join a stony path that winds down onto the mountain's superb western shoulder. The descent is steep but you are rewarded by wonderful views southeast across the cliffs, which are punctuated by precarious pillars of shattered rock. As you reach the bottom of the slope, keep to the cliff edge for more dizzying views of the apparently overhanging precipice.

Now drop across a stream and climb steeply onto a southern spur of Leahan. Follow the cliff edge before swinging northwest to reach the end of a rough track. This track leads around the bay with the fine, horseshoe beach of Trabane immediately ahead. You can either descend steep grassy slopes onto the sand, or continue along the track to reach the car park.

ROUTE 19:

Lavagh Beg and Lavagh More

Explore two scenic summits in the Blue Stack Mountains, passing numerous upland loughs and a 100m-high waterfall.

Grade:	4
Time:	3½–4½ hours
Distance:	8km (5 miles)
Ascent:	590m (1,940ft)
Map:	OSi 1:50,000 sheet 11

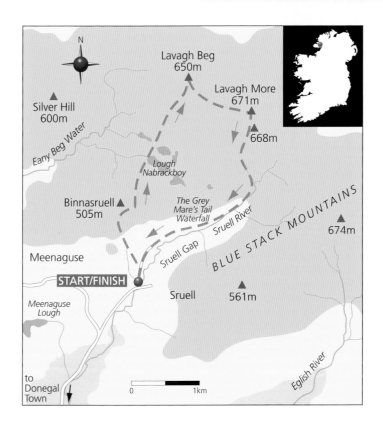

Start & Finish: The route starts and finishes at a small stone bridge over the Sruell River, at the southwestern end of the Sruell Valley (grid reference: G919887). From Donegal town, follow the N59 to a large roundabout on the western edge of town, then take the minor road signed for Letterbarra. Some 6km later, just before Letterbarra, turn right along a narrow road signed for the 'Bluestack Drive'. Continue for 7.5km to reach the mouth of the Sruell Valley. Turn right into the valley (the track marked on the OS map is in fact a paved road), and park beside the bridge about 1km further on.

The Croaghgorm or Blue Stack Mountains rise above Lough Eske, a few miles north of Donegal town. They are a wild, rough and beautiful range of granite summits, and give good views of the rest of Donegal. This route explores the Sruell Valley on the western side of the range, visiting the summits of Binnasruell (505m), Lavagh Beg (650m) and Lavagh More (671m). These stony peaks are interspersed by a liberal sprinkling of mountain loughs, while down in the valley, the 100m-high Grey Mare's Tail Waterfall is one of the most celebrated natural features in the area.

Though these mountains just miss out on being the highest in the range (Lavagh More is shorter than the tallest summit by a mere 3m), they are the most defined peaks, and progress is much easier here than across the rugged, hummocky ground further east. As with the rest of the range however, the ground drains poorly here, and can be rather boggy after rain. There are some small cliffs to avoid in poor visibility, but the relatively high starting point keeps the total ascent to a manageable 570m.

The Walk

From the bridge over the Sruell River, follow the road south for 100m and turn right onto a farm track. This brings you to some concrete animal pens after 100m; turn right here and follow the track through a metal gate. Continue along the track for 200m to the top of a small rise, where you should turn left and strike northwest across open ground. The track continues along the valley and will be followed on the return section of the route.

Climb over tussock-covered ground to reach the col between Binnasruell and a rise at 345m. Steep ground must now be negotiated to the north; pick your way carefully up the grass slopes, making sure to avoid steep cliffs to the east.

The gradient eases as you reach the top of Binnasruell. Veer west around the shore of Lough Anabrack, then pick your way northwest across undulating terrain strewn with peat hags and marshy hollows. Aim to join Lough Nabrackboy near its western shore. Cross the lake's outlet

Near the summit of Lavagh Beg in winter.

stream and continue ahead, passing between Loughs Nabrackbautia and Nagolan. The ground then steepens for the ascent to Lavagh Beg. The climb is steady all the way to the summit, where impressive views include Donegal Bay and Benbulbin to the south, and the Derryveagh Mountains to the north.

Descend southeast across a col, then begin the final ascent to Lavagh More. In places you will have to sidestep the weathered outcrops of granite that push through the grassy terrain. The summit of Lavagh More is marked by a cairn and more fine views east across the main Blue Stack range.

Cross to the southern edge of the small summit plateau, then begin to descend in a southwesterly arc. Steep cliffs to the south and southeast prevent a more direct line of descent. Join the banks of a small stream and follow this to its confluence with the main Sruell River, which is still just a stream itself at this height.

Follow the western bank of the river into the valley. Easier terrain can sometimes be found around 50m above the river rather than along the water's edge. After roughly 1km the Grey Mare's Tail Waterfall comes into sight above and to the right. This may be a trickle or a torrent depending on water levels, but the towering rock wall makes an impression at all times.

A fence stretches across the valley just south of the waterfall. Pass through a gate around 400m from the western bank of the river, then cross a field to reach a ruined stone building. As you progress, a track consolidates underfoot. This is the end of the same track you followed at the start of the day. Retrace your initial steps to return to the start of the circuit.

Benbulbin and Benwiskin

This varied route crosses Sligo's most famous mountains, offering thrilling views from long stretches of vertical escarpment.

Grade:	4
Time:	5–6 hours
Distance:	16.5km (10 miles)
Ascent:	670m (2,200ft)
Map:	OSi 1:50,000 sheet 16

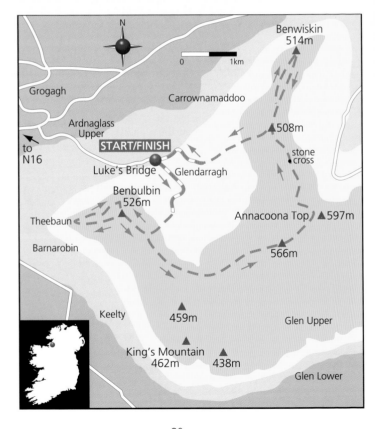

Start & Finish: The route starts and finishes at Luke's Bridge in Glendarragh (grid reference: G697473). Use the N16 to reach Mullaghnaneane church, 2km south of Grange. Turn east beside the church, then turn right at a crossroads 2km later. This lane may have a wire sheep fence stretched across it; continue ahead, having re-secured the fence. Park in a signed lay-by just before Luke's Bridge, where there is space for around eight cars.

Benbulbin and Benwiskin are the defining landmarks of County Sligo, and amongst the most distinctive peaks in Ireland. Reaching just 526m and 514m high, their unmistakable forms are rooted in shape, not height. Both are flat tabletop mountains, fringed by vertical escarpments over 100m high. Their cliffs have been chiselled to arrow-like points by the flowing movement of past ice sheets. Benbulbin is famed for its fantastic array of deep erosion gullies, while the undercut prow of Benwiskin rears up like a breaking wave perpetually ready to crash down into Donegal Bay. It's an exhilarating experience to stand on the edge of either precipice and admire the coastline below.

This route begins midway between the peaks, and begins with a steep ascent to the plateau that connects the two summits. Progress along the plateau is easier than you might expect, but the proliferation of sheer drops means vigilance is required in strong winds, and the route is best avoided altogether in poor visibility. If you are short of time, a simple out-and-back ascent of Benbulbin will take around three hours.

The Walk

Begin by crossing Luke's Bridge and heading southeast along the road. Ignore the first turn on the left; you will return this way at the end of the route. Climb steeply beside a tumbling stream, emerging into a wide upper valley beneath the peaks.

Around 800m from the start you arrive at a junction. Turn right across a concrete bridge and join a stony track. Keep right at the first fork after 20m, then turn left at another junction some 250m later. Continue for around 200m, then leave the track to the right and climb directly up the grassy slope ahead. The gradient is steep and sustained all the way to the top, but expanding coastal views compensate for the effort expended.

You may have to veer around some patches of scree shortly before you reach the top. Once on the plateau, turn right and head northwest along a broad ridge, following a grassy path underfoot. Within 500m you arrive at the trig pillar that marks the official summit of Benbulbin. The views are good, but the real climax is yet to come.

Continue west from the summit, passing several peculiar bog pools on your way to the apex of the mountain. The edges of the plateau taper inexorably inward until the ground disappears entirely, the sudden abyss filled by a sweeping panorama that extends from Mayo's Nephin Beg range

Looking over Donegal Bay from the precipitous prow of Benwiskin.

in the south to Donegal's Bluestack Mountains in the north. The exposure and the views are nothing short of sensational, but please remain mindful of the dangers whenever you are near the edge.

Turn right and follow the cliff line northeast for 1km, then climb back to the summit trig point. The route now begins a wide semicircular arc across the plateau towards Annacoona Top, at 597m. Retrace your steps southeast and continue over the rise at 500m. Descend across a wide hollow, then make a gradual climb northeast across grass and scattered rock.

A fence blocks your path just west of Annacoona Top, and little is gained by crossing it. Instead, turn left and approach the mountain's spectacular northern cliffs, which make a 200m vertical plunge to the valley of Gleniff below.

Turn left at the cliff edge. The next 3km are a delight, with fabulous views in all directions as you follow the cliff line north towards Benwiskin. After 400m you pass a tight cirque, where weathered pinnacles and the plunging cliff face combine in a dramatic amphitheatre.

Descend gradually along the clifftop, soon passing a Celtic cross set 150m back from the edge. Negotiate a swathe of peat hags in a shallow col, then cross point 508m. Around 500m later, veer left to approach Benwiskin's western cliffs. Here you'll be met by more stunning views and a heart-stopping perspective along the sharp rock fin of Benwiskin.

Head northeast along the clifftop until a fence bars the way. The tip of Benwiskin lies 200m further on, but you won't gain much by continuing. Instead, turn around and head back south. Keep to the ridge top and follow a faint track just right of a line of old fence posts to point 508m.

You can now begin the steady descent southwest into Glendarragh. Aim for a rough track that becomes visible below, crossing two wire fences before you reach it. Once at the track, turn right, with a stream on your left. The track turns to tarmac beside a bridge; continue straight ahead, still descending beside the stream. Follow the road as it sweeps left through a thicket of rhododendron to arrive back at Luke's Bridge.

Benwee Head

A remote and spectacular walk along an undulating cliff line, past islands, sea stacks and a 250m-high coastal precipice.

Grade:	4
Time:	4–5 hours
Distance:	12km (7½ miles)
Ascent:	480m (1,570ft)
Map:	OSi 1:50,000 sheets 22 and 23

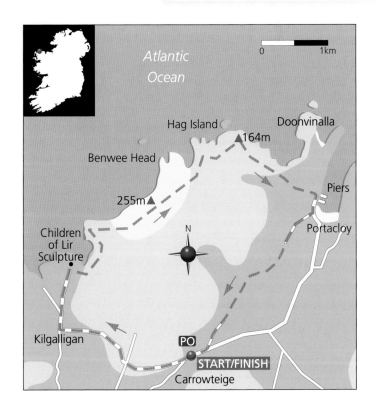

Start & Finish: The route starts and finishes beside the post office in the centre of Carrowteige village, at a car park marked by a walk information board (grid reference: F821420). This is a Gaeltacht region so Carrowteige is signed as *An Ceathrú Taidhg*. Follow signs north off the R314 from Glenamoy (Gleann na Muaidhe), around 21km northeast of Belmullet and 27km west of Ballycastle.

The north Mayo sea cliffs boast some of the most impressive coastal architecture in Ireland. The cliffs stretch for 30km between Rinroe Point and Belderg, and reach up to 300m high. The precipice has formed where coastal hills have been eroded by Atlantic swells, leaving vertical rock faces that are a literal cross-section of the mountains above. Just offshore, countless sea stacks, islands and rock arches litter the base of the crags. Little wonder that Robert Lloyd Praeger, in his seminal guidebook *The Way That I Went*, called this 'the finest piece of cliff scenery in the country'.

This is also an extremely remote area – the contrast could not be greater when compared to the Cliffs of Moher. However, two looped walks have been developed near the village of Carrowteige at the western end of the cliffs, and this makes a good base for your first excursion.

This route begins by following the waymarks along 3km of country road, then diverts east across Benwee Head, where the cliffs reach 255m high. After 6km of fabulous, wild coastal walking, you follow a series of bog tracks back to the start. As with all clifftop routes, please exercise extreme caution near the edge, and avoid walking in high winds or poor visibility.

The Walk

From the information board, head west and climb gently along the main road. You begin by following both the blue and red waymarkers, walking counter to the marked route. The red arrows turn right after 1km, but you should continue straight ahead, still following the blue symbols. The road begins to descend now, and brings you to a T-junction after another kilometre. Turn right here and follow a narrow lane north towards the coast.

You arrive at the coast beside a metal and stone sculpture that depicts the Children of Lir story. The sculpture is perched on the very edge of the clifftop, and there is an immediately striking view across the 100m-high cliffs that surround the inlet below. Turn right here and climb steeply east, again following the red markers. These signs will soon veer inland, but you should continue to follow the cliff line northeast across open, grassy ground.

Fine views west over Kid Island distract you from the steady climb to the 255m summit of Benwee Head. As well as the dizzying drop beneath your feet, the fabulous panorama now includes the Stags of Broadhaven,

Slieve League and Achill Island. Cross a fence as you start to descend, then continue northeast along the cliff line. Numerous islets lie just offshore here, with the towering stack of Hag Island prominent amongst them.

Descend around the bay of Doonvinalla and pass a steep, narrow promontory that once held an Iron Age fort. This is followed by a second headland distinguished by an old lookout building and the word EIRE written in stones on the ground. Both landmarks are relics of the Second World War.

The hamlet of Portacloy can now be seen to the south, at the back of a long, narrow bay. Descend towards the houses, crossing a stream and passing through a gate to reach the pier. Despite tracing the coastline for the past 6km, this is your first opportunity to reach the water's edge. There is a fine, sandy beach just east of the pier if you want a longer break.

From the pier, follow the road south for 200m to a junction. Turn right here, then keep left at the next fork. This lane heads southwest and soon turns into a track. Follow the track as it sweeps west and begins to climb, then look out for a gap in the bank on the left. The gap arrives around 1km from the fork, and is marked by an old waymarking post. Turn left here and make your way across 300m of open moorland before joining another bog track.

Follow this track southwest across the hillside to a house, where the surface becomes paved underfoot. Continue along the lane to a junction with the main road. Turn right here and complete the final 250m up the hill back to the start of the circuit.

Looking out from Doonvinalla towards Benwee Head.

Achill Head
and Croaghaun

A classic route over a truly
spectacular Atlantic summit,
above some of the highest sea
cliffs in Europe.

Grade:	4
Time:	5–6 hours
Distance:	13km (8 miles)
Ascent:	920m (3,020ft)
Map:	OSi 1:50,000 sheet 30

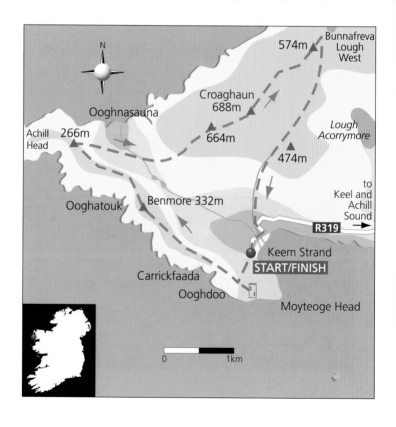

Start & Finish: The route starts and finishes at a large car park above Keem Strand (grid reference: F560042). Keem Strand is located at the end of the R319, the main road across Achill Island.

The great debate rages on: just where are the highest sea cliffs in Europe? In the west of Ireland, two coastal communities claim the bragging rights. Donegal's Slieve League awards itself the accolade, yet mighty Croaghaun on the western tip of Achill Island boasts cliffs that are both higher and marginally steeper. Yet the controversy misses the point: as coastal walks, both Slieve League *and* Croaghaun are unsurpassed in Europe for grandeur.

On Croaghaun, the erosive power of the Atlantic has chiselled away enough rock to create a 2km stretch of cliffs over 550m high. For walkers, the classic route starts from Keem Strand, taking in the view of Achill Head and the side profile of Croaghaun, before climbing to the 688m-high summit. Views over dramatic Bunnafreva Lough West and Lough Acorrymore return you neatly to Keem.

Another consequence of the mountain's steep coastal slopes are the oceanic winds, which often rise so abruptly that they form a persistent cap of cloud over the summit. It is worth waiting for clear, calm conditions, however, both to enjoy the fantastic views, and to avoid the inherent danger of walking above sheer cliffs in poor visibility. Also note that the path from Keem along the cliffs to Achill Head is not as significant as suggested by the OS map.

The Walk

The first obvious goal from Keem Strand is the lookout tower on Moyteoge Head. From the southern end of the car park, follow a steep, informal trail

Near the summit of Croaghaun, with Saddle Head beyond.

that climbs to the saddle just northwest of it. After visiting the tower, continue northwest, climbing steadily along the cliff edge across several small summits. The finest of these is at 332m, and affords dizzying views out to Achill Head.

Continue along the ridge to the base of Achill Head, where you are rewarded by a stunning profile of Croaghaun's western cliffs. The adventurous may want to add a side trip along the promontory of Achill Head; the very tip is accessible with some modest scrambling, but the extreme exposure restricts the outing to those with nerves of steel.

The route then descends east, dropping into a small river valley that contains the remains of the old booley settlement of Bunowna. Here, as many as sixteen oval-shaped huts used to serve as summer dwellings for shepherds while livestock were grazed and milked on the mountain. Beyond Bunowna, the steep western flank of Croaghaun must be faced almost head on. By traversing further southeast you gain slightly easier ground, but there is no avoiding the gradient in the last half of the climb, as you weave through large blocks and outcrops of rock to reach Croaghaun's western top at 664m.

The peak is located at the edge of the cliffs, and you are greeted by a sudden gut-wrenching view down vertiginous slopes that drop all the way to the Atlantic. To the northeast, 4km of dramatic cliffs stretch all the way to Saddle Head. Once you have recovered from the initial shock, you can also appreciate the wider 360° panorama, which encompasses much of the Mayo coastline.

Now follow the cliff line east, reaching the main summit of Croaghaun via a small saddle. The ridge is pleasantly exposed on both sides, with steep slopes sweeping away to the south towards Keem Strand. Beyond the main summit, descend along the cliff edge towards an obvious promontory, passing a section where a massive chunk of the cliff top is in the process of parting company with the rest of the mountain. The promontory provides a good perspective back across the summit of Croaghaun, and affords new views northeast across the deep corrie holding beautiful Bunnafreva Lough West.

From here, turn south and descend gently to the rim of the corrie holding Lough Acorrymore. The adjacent water treatment works means this lake provides water for the whole island. Pass around the top of the corrie, then continue southwest across Croaghaun's broad eastern spur. From the top of this shoulder, Keem Strand becomes visible below. Head for a strip of grass near the eastern edge of a small stream, which provides the easiest line of descent down the heather-clad slope and deposits you back at the car park where the route began.

ROUTE 23:
Minaun Heights

This accessible yet impressive trip involves some of the most scenic cliff walking in the country.

Grade:	4
Time:	4–5 hours
Distance:	13km (8 miles)
Ascent:	540m (1,770ft)
Map:	OSi 1:50,000 sheet 30

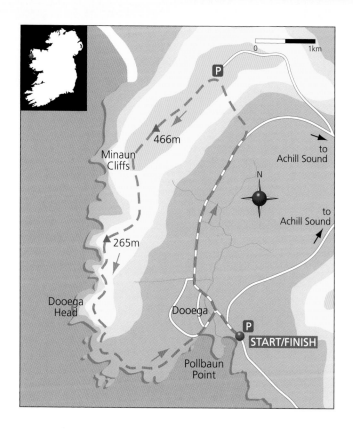

View over Achill Island from the Minaun Heights.

Start & Finish: The circuit starts and finishes at a car park above Camport Bay in Dooega village (grid reference: L675986). To reach Dooega, follow the R319 over Achill Sound towards Keel. Around 4km west of Achill Sound, turn left, following signs to Dooega (*Dumha Eige*). Turn left at the T-junction at the end of the road, and the car park is 300m later on the right.

If you have two vehicles, you can also start at the summit car park at the top of Minaun Heights (grid reference: F670028). To get there, turn left off the R319 5km west of Achill Sound, following the northernmost road to Dooega. Around 2km later, turn right up a steep lane signed to Minaun Heights.

In terms of coastal scenery, Achill Island is a walker's paradise. The most famous sea cliffs lie beneath Croaghaun, on the western tip of the island (see p. 86). But these are not the only cliffs on Achill, far from it. Though not as high as Croaghaun, the Minaun Heights are equally as impressive and far more accessible, and provide a wonderful viewpoint across the entire island.

There are two ways to complete this route. If you have two vehicles you can start at the summit car park and follow the cliffs downhill to Dooega, enjoying the rare pleasure of a route with 540m of descent but just 135m of ascent. Allow 3½ hours for this 9km route. With one vehicle, complete the full circuit as described below.

Given the proximity of sheer cliffs, it is best to avoid this route in poor visibility or high winds. Note too that the Minaun Heights are spelled Menawn on the OS map.

The Walk

From Camport Bay car park, turn left onto the road. Continue straight ahead across three road junctions in Dooega village, then begin to follow a minor road north beneath Minaun Heights. Continue along the road for around 3.5km, until you have passed the final house. The fence on the left stops just past this building. Turn west here and begin to climb directly up the steep heather-covered slope, aiming for the communication masts that mark Minaun's eastern summit.

A sustained ascent of 340 vertical metres brings you to the top, where you will find a large parking area. The view is immediately impressive, with the beach of Trawmore sweeping west to Croaghaun. Turn southwest at the car park and follow a stone track past the left side of a fenced building. The track weaves past various communication masts before coming to an end. Continue straight ahead over the peaty ground, climbing towards the prominent cairn and statue that mark the 466m summit.

Continue southwest from the summit, passing a series of small, modern cairns. Descend across broad slopes for around 800m, then swing east around an inlet to a col. Veer southwest here and climb a heather-covered slope to the top of the next rise, where you are rewarded by the first fantastic view north along the cliffs themselves.

Now you have joined the cliff line proper, it is essentially a case of tracing the edge of the cliffs around the western and southern reaches of Dooega Head. The terrain underfoot is a mixture of short heather and cropped grass, and a faint path is visible for most of the way.

The coastal scenery becomes more and more spectacular as you progress. First you round a series of small inlets where the rock drops 250m to the ocean. Then, as you near the tip of the headland, the focus suddenly switches to the south. The lighthouse and cliffs of Clare Island can now be seen 12km out to sea, backed by the myriad peaks of south Mayo and Connemara.

The cliffs begin to lose height now and a relatively steep heathery descent brings you almost down to sea level. Aim for an old stone wall that runs along the top of the shoreline, following this past several small fissures and rock arches.

Continue around the southeastern corner of the headland, passing between the wall and the shore. At times you may be forced onto the rocks themselves to avoid the occasional boggy patch. As you turn northeast towards Dooega a rough track begins to consolidate underfoot. Follow the track to a junction with a tarmac lane, and continue straight ahead along the road. Keep straight ahead at the first junction and turn right at the second, then walk the final 800m back to the car park.

Glendahurk Horseshoe

A fabulous mountain circuit that provides extensive views and includes a short but impressive rock arête.

Grade:	5
Time:	5–6 hours
Distance:	14.5km (9 miles)
Ascent:	980m (3,220ft)
Map:	OSi 1:50,000 sheets 30 and 31

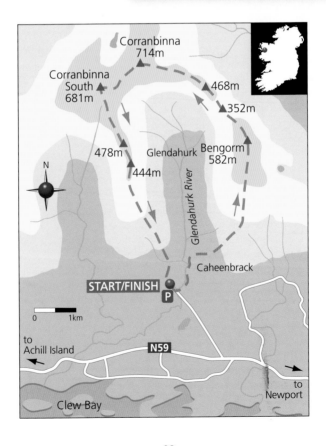

Start & Finish: The route starts and finishes at a parking area just north of the bridge in Glendahurk (grid reference: L911979). From Newport, follow the N59 west for 7km, then turn right onto a lane marked by an unobtrusive wooden sign for 'Carheenbrack' (the turn is located 100m east of a roadside statue of the Virgin Mary). Follow the lane for 2km and cross the bridge over the Glendahurk River. The gravel parking area is just beyond the bridge on the left, beside a junction of tracks.

The Nephin Beg Mountains of north Mayo are the most underrated range in Ireland. There are several wonderful hill-walks here, of a quality to rival any in the more popular regions of the country. A sense of remoteness still emanates from these peaks, and the lack of visitors is part of their attraction.

At 714m high, Corranbinna is not quite the highest peak in the range, but it is the most accessible and its coastal situation endows it with arguably the best views over north Mayo. It is the centrepoint of a horseshoe of mountains that surround the Glendahurk Valley, and provide the route for this walk. The circuit includes a traverse of a narrow rock ridge that is guaranteed to add excitement to the day. The exposure of this arête means it should be avoided in poor visibility or high winds.

The Walk

Begin by heading back south along the lane and recrossing the bridge over the Glendahurk River. Turn immediately left on the opposite bank and pass through a gate. Now follow the river upstream, keeping close to the banks to avoid marshy ground on the right. Several side streams are crossed via small wooden footbridges, and you will need to hop across a couple of ditches.

The ground now becomes rather boggy underfoot. This is the wettest terrain of the circuit, and will continue until you have climbed 100m or so up the slopes of Bengorm to the northeast. A stream can be seen cutting its way down from this peak to join the river, and the left bank provides as good an ascent route as any. The gradient is gentle and progress becomes easier as heather replaces the bog underfoot. The view from the top is fantastic, with the unmistakable shape of Croagh Patrick lying across Clew Bay to the south.

The descent north from Bengorm to the col is steep, and almost 200m is lost in height. Keep to the western side of the shoulder as the ground to the east is rockier and steeper still. Cross peat hags in the col, then climb across the two subsidiary peaks that lead towards Corranbinna. The ridge between Corranbinna and Corranbinna South is clearly silhouetted ahead, and from this angle its jagged form looks almost evil.

At the start of the Corranbinna Ridge, the crux of the route described.

The final col before the summit of Corranbinna reveals rock buttresses falling away vertically to the east. Keep to the left, away from this drop, during the final steep push to the top. The summit itself is a tight cone that provides a real sense of achievement. On a clear day the views stretch for over 100km in all directions. Notable landmarks can be identified across Donegal, Sligo and Mayo, while the intricate coastline and numerous islands stretch out into the Atlantic to the west.

Despite such fabulous views you will be drawn back to reality by the sight of the awesome ridge ahead. Descend steeply to meet the obstacle head on. The best option is to traverse along the top of the steep slope to the left of the knife-edged arête. The crest is broken in places, revealing terrifying but exhilarating glimpses of the land on the other side, hundreds of metres below. Keep to the left to skirt beneath some jagged pillars as you begin to climb again towards Corranbinna South. The ground remains very steep and continued attention is demanded. Finally you mount a rise and emerge onto the mountain's long, rounded summit, and can draw a deep breath of satisfied relief as you look back at the ground just crossed.

The descent from Corranbinna South is a long, gently graded one. Follow the ridge south until you are past point 444m. Here the shoulder pans out into wide slopes, and you should descend southwest across broken peat. The forest plantation in the centre of the horseshoe has been largely felled, but aim for its southernmost tip as marked on the map. Join a rough track and turn right, then turn left at a junction to return to the parking area.

Nephin

This short but rewarding
outing forges a direct path
to the second-highest
summit in Connacht.

Grade:	4
Time:	3–3½ hours
Distance:	6km (4 miles)
Ascent:	730m (2,400ft)
Map:	OSi 1:50,000 sheet 23 or 31

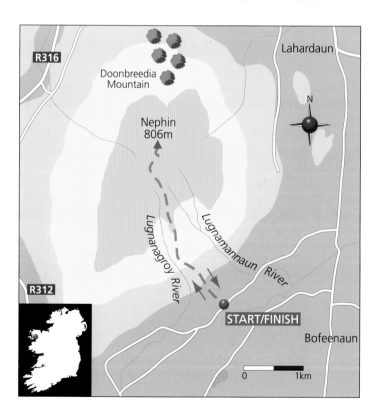

Start & Finish: The route starts and finishes along a minor road just southeast of Nephin, in the townland of Cloughbrack (grid reference: G115055). Access the area either from the R312 Castlebar–Bangor road, or the R315 Crossmolina–Pontoon road, using your OS map to help you find the right turn-off. The start is located around 800m west of a water treatment works, which can be seen on the lower slopes of the mountain. Look along the northern side of the road for a stone-clad cottage with a farmyard behind it. Tracks lead off on both sides of the cottage, and this route starts up the track to the right. Parking is restricted to roadside spaces, but please be careful to avoid blocking any entrances.

Nephin is a perfect winter mountain. The views from the isolated summit are far-ranging, and, at 806m high, there is the additional satisfaction of reaching the second-highest point in Connacht. Yet the trip to the top is short and uncomplicated, taking most people less than four hours. When limited daylight hours restrict your options in terms of mountain routes, there is always enough time for a quick jaunt up the side of Nephin.

This out-and-back route approaches the peak along its southeastern flank, where two steep gullies are bisected by a narrow ridge. The route itself is relatively straightforward, though it does involve 730m of unrelenting ascent. Avoid walking in poor visibility, when great care is needed to locate the correct line of descent. The outing starts along a farm track and the landowner is very friendly, though if he is nearby it is only polite to let him know your intentions before you head out across his land.

The Walk

Begin by heading along the track on the right-hand side of the cottage. This carries you northwest past a series of fields. As you progress, survey the slopes ahead. Two streams cut deep gullies into the side of the mountain, with a narrow ridge climbing between them. Your aim is to ascend and descend along the crest of this ridge.

Pass through a wire gate at a corner in the track, then continue to a fence that marks the farm's upper boundary. Climb carefully over the fence and you will find yourself out on the open mountainside. The terrain across the lower section is tough-going, with steep slopes clad in thick heather and grass. Reassure yourself that this is the roughest part of the route, and the ground will become easier underfoot within 100m or so of vertical ascent.

Either head directly up the slope or, for a more interesting variation, veer west slightly to reach the edge of the Lugnagroy River gully. From the high banks of this wild little stream, you can gaze up at the steep falls and pools and imagine the power of the water after heavy rain.

Climbing the slopes of Nephin in winter.

Veer north away from the river and climb onto the ridge itself. Follow the crest of the ridge up the shoulder between the two gullies. The vegetation has now died back underfoot, and relatively short grass covers the peaty slopes. Halfway up you should make the most of a brief respite in the gradient, because it is not long before the slope steepens once again for the final push to the top. As you gain height, rocks and stones become increasingly common underfoot, and ever more expansive views encourage you upward. Obvious landmarks include Lough Conn to the east, and the unmistakable cone of Croagh Patrick across Clew Bay to the southwest.

The ridge joins the summit plateau around 250m southwest of a cairn topped by a flag. Though not directly on the route, the cairn provides a useful marker in poor visibility. As the ridge eases onto the stony plateau, the views suddenly open out around you. You can now appreciate Nephin's magnificent 360° panorama for the first time. On a clear day the cliffs of Slieve League of Donegal are visible to the north, while the Nephin Beg Mountains stand out to the west.

Turn northeast and head along the plateau to reach the large trig point at its northern tip. If visibility is poor, please exercise extreme caution on your final approach to the summit because the ground disappears into a precipitous corrie just a few metres north of the trig pillar. In clear conditions, more great views include a fine perspective along Lough Conn.

The descent is simply a matter of reversing your outward route back to the farm below.

ROUTE 26:
Clare Island

A 462m summit, tremendous coastal views and impressive vertical sea cliffs are all features of Ireland's most mountainous island.

Grade:	4
Time:	5–6 hours
Distance:	15km (9½ miles)
Ascent:	600m (1,970ft)
Map:	OSi 1:50,000 sheet 30

Walker beside Clare Island Lighthouse, heading along the island's northern sea cliffs.

Start & Finish: The route starts and finishes at Clare Island pier (grid reference: L715852). Clare Island Ferries (Tel: 098 23737; www.clareislandferry.com) and O'Malley Ferries (Tel: 098 25045; www.omalleyferries.com) both operate between Roonagh Quay and Clare Island. The crossing costs €15 return, and takes around 20 minutes. Both companies offer daily sailings all year round – contact the operators for full schedule information. Roonagh Quay is situated around 28km west of Westport, via the R335 through Lousiburgh.

Standing guard at the mouth of Clew Bay in County Mayo, Clare Island is a rugged, cliff-fringed outpost that extends to 10 square kilometres. Dominated by Knockmore (462m), it is the most mountainous of all the islands of Ireland, and boasts the sort of walking that is normally associated with hilly regions on the mainland. Here, however, the combination of height and island location means that walkers are rewarded by coastal views from a unique perspective. Add several kilometres of impressive vertical sea cliffs and throw in a little island atmosphere, and you have a truly tremendous Atlantic outpost to explore.

To get the best from the island, you really need to gain a perspective over the northwest coast. Here, beneath the summit of Knockmore, sheer cliffs drop some 400m to the waves below. The route described here makes the most of this dramatic scenery, and follows quiet laneways at the start and finish to allow you to complete a full circumnavigation of the island.

The existence of precipitous drops means you should avoid the section along the cliffs in poor visibility and high winds.

The Walk

From the ferry pier in Fawnglass, walk around the harbour and pass a tower house that once served as a castle for the pirate queen Grace O'Malley. Turn right and follow a small road around the back of the sandy beach, which is a focal point of activity during the summer. Keep left at a road junction in front of the community centre, following signs for the lighthouse. The lane passes through several gateways with adjacent stiles as it climbs across a modest spur, then winds across two further rises.

Around 2km from Fawnglass, the road comes to another junction. Turn right here and begin a steady climb that continues all the way to the northern tip of the island. The road dwindles to a single-lane track as you near the coast, and the scenery becomes progressively wilder. A final push brings you to the lighthouse, which dates from 1806 and is the only double-towered lighthouse in Ireland. The light was decommissioned in 1965 because its location, perched on the cliff edge some 100m above the water, meant it was often shrouded in mist.

This is a good vantage point from which to appreciate the sheer cliffs that stretch away to the west. From the lighthouse, head southwest across open ground and begin to follow the cliff edge, staying on the landward side of a fence. Cropped grass and firm turf ease your passage over a series of short but steep undulations, with the fine views over Knockmore and the sea cliffs providing constant distraction. The route swings west as you progress onto the east ridge of Knockmore and begin the unrelenting climb to the top. Rougher terrain and tussock grass take over underfoot as you gain height, and you may need to veer inland slightly over the steepest sections. Fortunately, views from the summit trig pillar more than justify the effort of the ascent; the panorama includes the islands of Inishturk and Inishbofin to the south, as well as the mainland mountains of Connemara, Mayo and Achill Island.

From the summit, head southwest across the broad, peaty summit ridge, passing a large stone cairn on the way. Now descend steeply from the edge of the plateau, following a shoulder southwest towards the road and bungalows below. As you descend, the ruins of a Napoleonic signal tower can be seen near the northwestern tip of the island. This provides an easy detour for those with the energy – a track then leads from the tower to the end of the road.

Back on the main circuit, join the road and turn left. It is now a simple matter of following the tarmac back to Fawnglass. The 5.5km journey is enlivened by good views of the Mayo coastline and a chance to visit the Cistercian abbey, which contains rare medieval wall-paintings and lies on the left side of the road about halfway back.

Inishturk

Explore a modest
mountain summit and
130m-high sea cliffs on the
circumnavigation of this
charming Atlantic island.

Grade:	3
Time:	3½–4½ hours
Distance:	10km (6 miles)
Ascent:	290m (950ft)
Map:	OSi 1:50,000 sheet 37

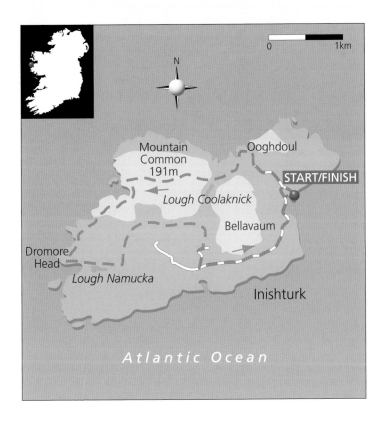

Start & Finish: The route starts and finishes at Inishturk pier (grid reference: L620749). O'Malley Ferries (Tel: 098 25045; www.omalleyferries.com) have regular services to Inishturk from Roonagh Quay. The crossing costs around €20 return, and takes roughly 40 minutes. There are daily sailings all year round – contact the operator for full schedule information. Roonagh Quay is located around 28km west of Westport, via the R335 through Lousiburgh.

Looking along Inishturk's north coast to Mountain Common.

I nishturk is one of the most remote inhabited islands in Ireland, lying 10km off the shore of County Mayo. Yet this Atlantic outpost provides a perfect mixture of wild scenery and welcoming hospitality, with sandy bays, a modest mountain summit and 130m-high sea cliffs thrown in for good measure.

The scenery is impressive without being unduly demanding, and the island's 60 per cent of commonage means walkers can wander freely over much of the land. There are two signed loop walks, and this route follows the markers at the beginning and end of the circuit. However, on the island's wilder western side, it diverts off the signed trail to visit its finest natural features: the summit of a 191m-high hill, and a stretch of soaring cliff line.

The open ground consists of a mixture of cropped grass and exposed rock outcrops, providing a firm surface that is perfect for walking. The only proviso is that much of the route passes along exposed cliffs, so care is needed near the edge. Avoid walking in poor visibility and high winds.

The Walk

From the ferry pier, walk to the harbour entrance and join the only real road on the island. Some 300m later you reach a junction. Turn right here and follow this lane for 500m. Now pass through a metal gate and join a rough stone track that crosses the rock-studded commonage ahead.

Though you will return to the track shortly, begin by detouring north to the coast. Turn right just inside the gate and follow a wall to the top of an 80m-high chasm known as Ooghdoul. This provides an impressive introduction to the island's wild side, and during the breeding season you should see fulmars and their chicks nesting on the ledges below.

Turn left at the chasm and begin to follow the coastline southwest. There are good views across the bay to the hill of Mountain Common, which is topped by the prominent ruins of a signal tower. The easiest way to reach this summit is via the stone track. Swing back south across rocky ground, then rejoin the track and turn right.

Climb gently along the track, past Lough Coolaknick. Just beyond this lough, turn right across open ground. A steady climb brings you to the top of Mountain Common, the highest point of the island at 191m. The summit is marked by a trig point and a Napoleonic signal tower, as well as fine views across Achill Island, Clare Island and the mainland mountains of Connemara and Mayo.

From the summit, head west across a series of hummocks to reach the coast. The cliffs here are the highest on the island, dropping vertically for 130m to the waves below. The sense of space and power is quite exhilarating.

Now turn left and begin to follow the coastline south. Descend gradually past several more chasms and viewpoints. Cross two streams, then climb slightly to reach Dromore Head. This final promontory provides a fine view south to the island of Inishbofin.

Turn inland at Dromore Head and head east along the side of an inlet. Pass Lough Namucka and continue east until you meet a stone wall. Turn left here and follow the wall north for 600m to a corner. Turn right here, still following the wall, and head east for 1.5km to reach a gravel road.

You join the road beside the island's Irish football pitch, a wonderfully rugged playing field that has been squeezed onto one of the only flat spots on the island. Turn right onto the road and continue to a junction with the coast road 1km later. Turn left here and begin to follow this road back towards the harbour.

If you have time to spare, it is worth making a short detour near the top of the hill before the final descent to the pier. Pass through a metal gate on the right, following a sign for Tranaun. Descend across a field to reach a delightful sandy cove, which provides a perfect place to cool off on a hot day. Then return to the road for the final 800m back to the pier.

ROUTE 28:
Croagh Patrick

A high-quality route that traverses the Croagh Patrick massif; the connoisseur's way to appreciate Ireland's holy mountain.

Grade:	4
Time:	4–5 hours
Distance:	10km (6 miles)
Ascent:	960m (3,149ft)
Map:	The route straddles four OSi 1:50,000 sheets – numbers 30, 31, 37 and 38.

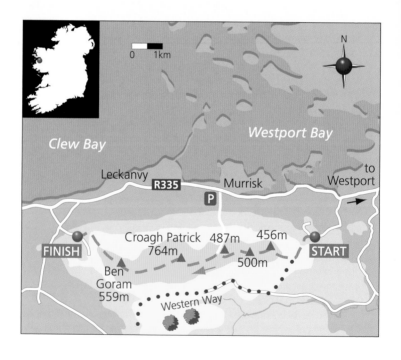

Reflection of Croagh Patrick from Murrisk.

Start & Finish: The route starts at the bottom of a track at grid reference: L949809. From Westport, head west along the R335 towards Louisburg. After 5km, and immediately after Belclare bridge, turn left onto a minor road. Follow the marker posts for the Western Way, bearing right at a fork after 1km. A kilometre later, park beside a gated track that climbs off to the left, and is marked by walking posts. This is enough space for two vehicles.

The walk finishes along a minor road west of Croagh Patrick at grid reference: L875808. From Belclare bridge, continue west along the R335. Around 1.5km west of Leckanvy village, turn left onto a road signed for Chris Harper Art Studio. Follow this road for 1km, then turn left. Park around 1km later, in a small layby just before a high stone wall that spans either side of the road.

Croagh Patrick is perhaps the most famous and definitely the most climbed mountain in Ireland. It attracts around a million walkers annually, some 25,000 of them congregating on Reek Sunday, the traditional day of pilgrimage on the last Sunday in July. The summit holds the remains of a prehistoric settlement dating from 300 BC, while some 700 years later, St Patrick is said to have fasted on the summit for forty days and forty nights.

Croagh Patrick makes for a great walk. Rising directly from the southern shore of Clew Bay, the 764m-high summit is a superlative vantage point. The most common way up the mountain is an out-and-back trip along the tourist path from Murrisk; this 8km route takes three hours to complete. However, the path's breadth, popularity and unrelenting steepness leads hillwalkers who prefer more natural surrounds to look for an alternative approach. The traverse of the entire Croagh Patrick massif, as described here, gives the fullest, most satisfying experience possible.

Unfortunately the A-to-B format means that two cars or a cooperative driver are a prerequisite. Alternatively, consider an out-and-back ascent from the end of the route to the summit. Though you will be retracing your steps, this route is far more satisfying than the battle up the tourist path.

The Walk

Pass through the gate and begin to climb along the track; waymarking posts indicate that this is the route of the Western Way. After 700m you pass over the brow of the ridge. Just after the track starts to descend, cross a wooden stile on the right, which is marked as part of the 61km Croagh Patrick Heritage Trail. The marked trail heads north around the base of the mountains, but you should veer diagonally left, climbing over rough, heathery slopes towards the hilltop ahead.

Cross a stone wall where a gap has formed and continue climbing, keeping to the shoulder and aiming for a minor summit. From here, fine views stretch across Clew Bay to the north, a panorama that only improves as you progress further.

Continue west, keeping to the tops across several intermittent rises. The thick heather underfoot can make for heavy going, and you may be tempted to join a narrow peat path that contours around the southern side of the last rise. This leads to a junction with the tourist path from Murrisk. This rough, stony trail is as wide as a country lane in some places, and comes as quite a shock after the previous wild terrain.

Follow the tourist path as it makes an unrelenting ascent over 300 vertical metres of steep, loose stones. Depending on the time of year, this part of the route may be busy with people. The mountain's first pilgrim station is passed near the start of the climb, with a plaque prescribing an impressive list of rituals to be performed by the devout.

Around forty minutes of uphill grind should bring you to the top. The summit of Croagh Patrick is cluttered with buildings, makeshift shelters and a second pilgrim station, and often crowded with people too. The current church dates from 1905 and is the highest church in Ireland. Yet there is no denying the natural splendour of the view – see if you can count the myriad islands of Clew Bay, which are said to number one for every day of the year.

It is something of a relief to leave the hustle of the summit and continue west, instantly leaving the crowds behind. Follow a small stone path that descends steeply to *Reilig Mhuire* (the Virgin's cemetery), the third and last pilgrim station and possibly a pre-Christian burial site.

Continue across a peat col then veer northwest, climbing the modest distance to Ben Goram (559m), the final peak of the route. Now begin to descend northwest, keeping to the top of the ridge to avoid precipitous slopes to the west. Continue past a prominent pillar-like cairn, and when the gradient eases near the base of the slope, veer left towards a high stone wall that spans either side of the road below. Cross a wooden stile just right of the wall; your transport should be waiting nearby.

Mweelrea

Two airy ridges and incredible coastal views make this one of Ireland's finest mountain walks.

Grade:	5
Time:	6–7 hours
Distance:	15km (9½ miles)
Ascent:	1,070m (3,510ft)
Map:	OSi 1:50,000 sheet 37

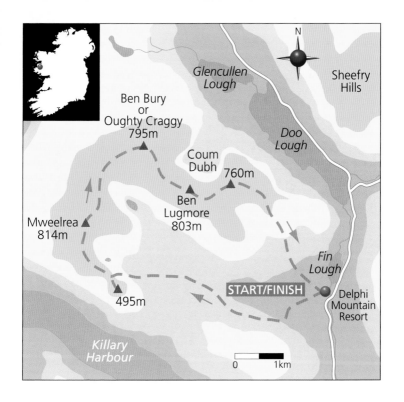

Looking back along the ridge towards Mweelrea from Ben Lugmore.

Start & Finish: The route starts and finishes at Delphi Mountain Resort, 5km south of Doo Lough along the R335 (grid reference: L 840652). Join the R335 in either Louisburgh to the north, or Leenane to the south. Note that Delphi is a private hotel not a public car park – large groups should use the lay-bys around Doo Lough and shuttle walkers to Delphi from there.

If I were pressed to come up with a list of my favourite mountain walks in Ireland, this horseshoe circuit on Mweelrea would probably make it into the top three. At 814m Mweelrea is Connacht's highest summit; an engaging and complex mountain with so many ridges and subsidiary peaks that there are almost endless possibilities for exploration.

There are several quality routes up the mountain, including an ascent from the northern shore of Doo Lough through atmospheric Coum Dubh, passing over the exhilarating terrain of The Ramp. However, the scenic variety and topographic purity of this horseshoe makes it probably the most satisfying route of all.

Remember that there are no easy routes on Mweelrea: it is a big mountain surrounded by a great deal of difficult and dangerous ground. Save the trip for clear conditions, and make sure to leave enough time to get down in daylight.

The Walk

From Delphi car park, look for a gravel track that passes around the right-hand side of the hotel building. Follow this onto a track that veers right into the forest, then begins to run along the southern side of the Owennaglogh River. Keep right at several track junctions and stay beside the river as you cross a large clearing. Just before you enter the next band of trees, turn left at a track junction, and then keep left again at the following junction. This trail leads out to the southern boundary of the forest, then swings right and begins to descend along the western edge of the trees.

At this point the track disappears into the bog and you have a choice to make. In wet conditions it is best to traverse across the rough hillside, heading directly towards the unnamed summit at 495m. In dry conditions it is easier to trace the banks of the Owennaglogh and Sruhaunbunatrench rivers to reach the col between point 495m and the southeastern shoulder of Mweelrea.

Whichever route you choose, it is worth climbing to the top of point 495m to appreciate the fine views across Mweelrea's magnificent east face. Now descend northwest to the col and begin the climb up the shoulder. As you gain height the terrain becomes easier underfoot, through the gradient is steep at times. There is a brief respite near the 700m contour, where a great cleft cuts into the shoulder.

Above the cleft the ridge swings north, and the slopes converge in an airy arête that feels almost alpine in nature. Follow the apex of the ridge and make the final, steep climb to the top. The summit itself is curiously flat, adorned with a modest cairn perched on the very edge of the east face. Along with sensational coastal views, the impressive vista includes the Twelve Bens and the Maumturks to the south.

Descend northeast to a col, then climb to the summit of Ben Bury, which is steeply cut on its northern side. Now descend southeast to reach a cairn in the gap between Ben Bury and the Ben Lugmore ridge. This cairn marks the top of The Ramp, which plunges east down into Coum Dubh.

Continue southeast along the crest of the ridge, now passing over along the most entertaining and exhilarating terrain on the mountain. A faint path means progress is surprisingly straightforward despite the rocks and occasional exposure. Ben Lugmore (803m) is the penultimate summit on the ridge. From here you drop down into a grassy gap and then climb a short distance to an unnamed top. Now turn northeast and enjoy more excellent, easy walking along a broader ridge to point 760m.

At the end of the ridge, turn southeast and follow an easy ridge down towards the Delphi Mountain Resort. A straightforward descent deposits you on some rough and boggy ground in the Owennaglogh Valley. Follow an old boundary wall towards Delphi. Just before the buildings you must ford the Owennaglogh River, a simple task in normal water levels, but probably impossible in flood. If you are stuck there are two iron girders carrying a water pipe that will suffice as a makeshift bridge. All that remains is to cross a fence and follow a forestry track the short distance back to Delphi.

Sheeffry Traverse

This ridge-top traverse of the Sheeffry massif is one of the most scenic hill-walks in Ireland.

Grade:	4
Time:	4–5 hours
Distance:	11km (7 miles)
Ascent:	700m (2,300ft)
Map:	OSi 1:50,000 sheet 37

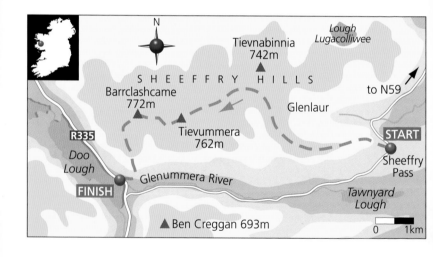

Start & Finish: The walk starts at the top of Sheeffry Pass (grid reference: L922686). From Westport, head 8km south along the N59 to the village of Carney. Turn west here along a narrow road signed to Sheeffry Pass. Follow this for 12km to reach the pass, where limited parking is available in lay-bys beside the road. More space can be found in a parking area 1km west of the pass.

To reach the end of the route, continue southwest along the road for a further 8km to a junction with the R335. Turn right here for 300m and park in a small lay-by just north of the Glenummera River (grid reference: L845677).

I f a competition were held to find the most scenic mountain ridge in Ireland, the Sheeffry Hills would be in contention for a medal. Sandwiched between Clew Bay and Connemara, the diversity of topography visible from the route is simply amazing. Isolation and solitude are another a defining characteristic of these hills, and on a clear day the route exemplifies the very essence of Irish hillwalking.

The walk described here traverses the main Sheeffry ridge, which stretches for 5km above 700m high. Steep corries have been carved into either side of the massif, and a narrow col towards the western end is particularly exhilarating. The defined topography makes route finding relatively straightforward, though the abrupt edges to the plateau mean you should avoid walking in poor visibility. Note too that the OS map marks the main peaks by height, but not name.

The only potentially problematic part of the route is organising transport. Some 8km of road separate the start and finish, requiring two vehicles, a bike or accommodating driver. Alternatively, consider completing the Glenlaur horseshoe at the eastern end of the range – climb as described to the summit of Tievnabinnia (742m), then return along the mountain's western ridge. Allow 4½-5½ hours for this fine, 10km circuit with 760m ascent.

Enjoying the view north towards Croagh Patrick from Tievnabinnia.

The Walk

From Sheeffry Pass, head west towards a small pine plantation. A fence stretches uphill beyond the trees; follow along the right-hand side of this, climbing across grassy terrain, which can be wet in places. In less than a kilometre you arrive at the top of the first rise, where there are impressive views northeast into the steep-sided basin of Glenlaur.

Now follow the ridgeline west and then northwest. The ground undulates over several intermittent rises, with short grass underfoot making for relatively easy progress. The fence continues to mark the crest for some distance, providing a handy navigation guide before it disappears south.

Negotiate several small peat hags, then make the final, steady ascent to the summit plateau, taking care to avoid steep ground to the west. If you want to visit Tievnabinnia (742m), continue north over the rock-strewn plateau to reach the small summit cairn. Many walkers will be happy to cut the corner and join the summit ridge around 800m west of Tievnabinnia. The impact of the view to the north is the same; impressively sheer corrie walls fall away beneath your feet, backed by the distinctive profile of Croagh Patrick. Beyond that lies Clew Bay, with Clare Island and Achill Island standing sentinel at its entrance.

Now follow the ridge southwest past a series of pools and small loughs. A gentle, grass-covered slope leads to the concrete trig pillar at the top of Tievummera (762m), where more splendid views are revealed across the serrated skyline of Connemara to the south.

Continue on from the summit, arcing southwest then northwest around the lip of a steep corrie. The narrowest part of the ridge can now be seen ahead, marking the col beneath Barrclashcame. The ground remains wide enough to preclude any real danger, but steep drops either side ensure at least a little excitement. A final short climb then brings you to the top of Barrclashcame (772m). From here the bulk of Mweelrea – Connacht's highest mountain – fills your vision to the west, while the waters of Killary Harbour can be seen to the south.

Veer southwest at the summit of Barrclashcame and continue to the end of the plateau, taking care in poor visibility to avoid steep cliffs to the west. The easiest line of descent now lies to the south. Drop steeply but steadily down the grassy slope, skirting several rock outcrops on the way. As you near the valley, veer west towards Doo Lough, aiming to join the road at the western end of a copse of Scots pine. Your vehicle should not be far away.

ROUTE 31:

Ben Creggan and Ben Gorm

A relatively strenuous route over three distinct summits, offering great views and good ridge walking.

Grade:	5
Time:	5–6 hours
Distance:	12km (7½ miles)
Ascent:	1,060m (3,480ft)
Map:	OSi 1:50,000 sheet 37

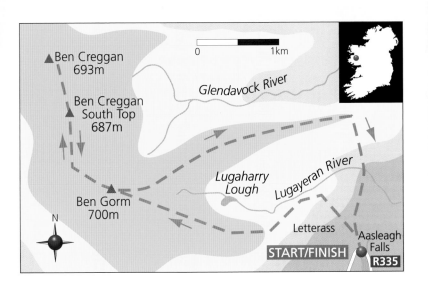

Looking back along the ridge to Ben Creggan and Ben Gorm.

Start & Finish: The walk starts and finishes beside Aasleagh Falls, at the northern tip of Killary Harbour (grid reference: L894644). The waterfall is a natural landmark, and located along the R335. Access the area via the N59 Westport–Leenane road, and turn north onto the R335 about 3.5km north of Leenane. Ample roadside lay-bys offer plenty of parking space just west of the falls.

Just east of Mweelrea lies a trio of summits, which are often overlooked but provide incredible views of most of Connemara and south Mayo. The mountains in question are Ben Gorm (700m), Ben Creggan South Top (687m) and Ben Creggan (693m). Apart from superlative views, these peaks boast several sharp ridges and deep corries. Two such ridges are followed on the ascent and descent; in some places the exposure is enough to provide an excitingly airy feel, though the ground is never narrow enough to be worrying.

The route involves a bit of backtracking, but this is worth it to avoid the boggy ground in Glendavock, and to access the fine descent ridge. Groups with two cars could just as easily start at the southern end of Doo Lough and climb the steep northern slope of Ben Creggan before traversing the three summits and descending to Aasleagh Falls. Whichever option you choose, try to wait for clear conditions to enjoy the fantastic views, and to avoid the difficult and potentially hazardous task of navigating the route in poor visibility.

The Walk

From the parking lay-bys, walk along the road towards the Erriff River. Just before the bridge, cross a stile on the left and follow a riverside path towards Aasleagh Falls. This picturesque drop gained international fame when it featured in Jim Sheridan's 1990 film *The Field*. Climb the stile beside the cascade, then turn immediately left. Cross a lane and continue uphill with a fence on your left. The ground here is covered by thick tussock grass but progress becomes easier as you gain height.

Follow the fence as it veers west and arrives at a boggy dip on the ridge. From here there is a great view across the deep, cliff-fringed corrie that falls some 200m from the summit of Ben Gorm. Now turn west and begin to climb the mountain's curving southwest ridge. The walking is delightful as you weave around small outcrops and enjoy increasingly expansive views behind.

After a couple of steep sections flanked by big drops into the corrie on the right, the ridge flattens out onto an eroded plateau strewn with rocks and peat hags. In poor visibility navigational difficulties begin here, and it could be problematic finding the summit cairn. There are actually two cairns, with a flatter subsidiary cairn located about 100m east of the main cairn. In clear weather the view is so impressive it is hard to decide where to look first. The southern vista, across Killary Harbour to the Maumturk and Twelve Ben Mountains, is perhaps most compelling.

You also have a good view north across the route's remaining two peaks. Begin by descending northwest for a few hundred metres, then turn north and follow a broad ridge into a grassy col. Bypass a small rock outcrop and climb steeply for a short distance to reach Ben Creggan South Top, which is marked by a small cairn.

A smaller and narrower gap now lies between you and the marginally higher summit of Ben Creggan. Descend steeply and then climb the short distance to the summit cairn. The views from here are just as impressive as those from Ben Gorm, with Mweelrea, Doo Lough and Sheeffry Hills taking centre stage to the north and west.

When you are ready, retrace your steps across Ben Creggan South Top to Ben Gorm's summit cairn. Now head east to join the ridge that forms the northern arm of the Lugaharry corrie. Take extreme care here in poor visibility; there are precipitous drops to the north before you reach the ridge, and steep ground on either side once the descent begins. In good conditions the trip along the arête is enjoyably airy, and provides a memorable finale to the route.

Continue to a col between the main ridge and point 356m. Now turn south and descend over what may be quite wet ground to reach the Lugayeran River. A short climb now brings you back to the base of the ridge from which you approached Ben Gorm. Descend along the fence to Aasleagh Falls and the end of the route.

ROUTE 32:
Diamond Hill

A short, signed trail leads to the top of this compact peak for great views across Connemara National Park.

Grade:	2
Time:	2½–3 hours
Distance:	7km (4½ miles)
Ascent:	420m (1,380ft)
Map:	OSi 1:50,000 sheet 37, or Harvey Superwalker 1:30,000 *Connemara*.

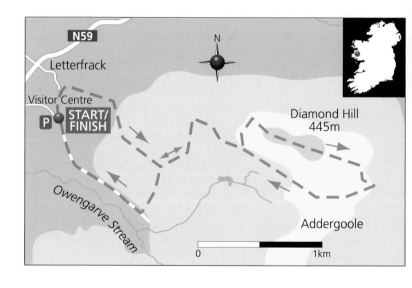

Now head south along a rough path. The trail soon crosses the line of the Dingle Way, and the junction is marked by a black waymarking post. To the southeast the narrow portal that guards the entrance to Derrymore Glen is clearly visible; you will exit through this gap at the end of the route.

The first challenge is the ascent of Gearhane, which lies directly ahead. This initial slope is very steep and covered in heather, and the effort is sustained all the way to the top. Once at the apex of the ridge you are rewarded by wonderful views, over both Tralee Bay to the north and into Derrymore Glen below. There is also a clear view around the remainder of the circuit ahead.

At the ridgeline, turn right. The gradient is easier now, and short, rock-studded grass makes for easier progress. The summit of Gearhane (792m) is unmarked except for several sandstone outcrops, but there is a fine view along the length of the Dingle Peninsula to Brandon Mountain at its western tip.

Continue to follow the ridgeline around the southwestern corner of the horseshoe. A gradual climb leads to the top of 835m Caherconree, which is marked by a cairn and more fine views south towards the MacGillycuddy's Reeks.

The descent from this peak requires care because there is a precipitous drop to the north. Head east and join a path across a grassy ridge little more than a metre wide. This brings you down to a broad col strewn with maroon-coloured sandstone rocks. Now climb steadily northeast to reach Baurtregaum, whose rounded summit is crowned by a trig point and surrounding ring cairn.

From Baurtregaum, turn northwest and head towards the shoulder marked on the map as point 723m. Curve gradually west then southwest as you descend. Your target is Derrymore Lough in the glen below, and the slightly circuitous approach is designed to avoid steep slopes above the lough's southwestern shore.

The deep amphitheatre of upper Derrymore Glen is a marked contrast to the airy exposure of the summits, and it is well worth pausing on the shore of the lough to soak up the full atmosphere of the place. When you are ready, begin to follow the Derrymore River north along the base of the valley. Negotiate a relatively steep drop beneath the lough, then join an intermittent path along the western bank of the river. You will cross several patches of wet ground as you descend, but the chutes and pools of the stream provide a pleasant distraction.

Pass around the lower slopes of Gearhane and follow the path out of the glen. Keep alongside the main river and descend gradually north to meet the Dingle Way at a wooden footbridge and marker post. Turn left here and follow the Dingle Way for 200m to the junction you passed on your outward journey. Now turn right and retrace your initial steps back to the start.

ROUTE 42:
Coomloughra Horseshoe

With sharp ridges, airy views and the three highest summits in the country, this challenging route is perhaps the finest mountain horseshoe in Ireland.

Grade:	5
Time:	6–7 hours
Distance:	13.5km (8½ miles)
Ascent:	1,200m (3,940ft)
Map:	OSi 1:50,000 sheet 78, OSi 1:25,000 *MacGillycuddy's Reeks*, or Harvey Superwalker 1:30,000 *MacGillycuddy's Reeks*.

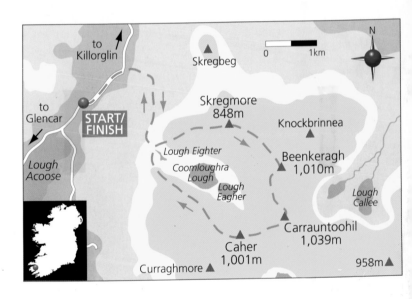

ROUTE 39:

Great Blasket Island

An evocative circuit
through a deserted
village and along the
mountainous spine
of this wild Atlantic
outpost.

Grade:	3
Time:	3–3½ hours
Distance:	9km (5½ miles)
Ascent:	450m (1,480ft)
Map:	OSi 1:50,000 sheet 70

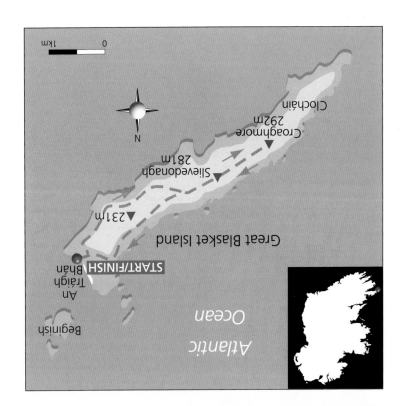

Atlantic
Ocean

Beginish

An
Tráigh
Bhán

START/FINISH

Great Blasket Island

▼231m

Slievedonagh
281m ▼

Croaghmore
292m
Clocháin ▼

N

0   1km

Start & Finish: The route starts and finishes at the landing stage on Great Blasket Island (grid reference: V281977). Several operators provide regular ferry services to the island between Easter and September. The shortest crossing leaves from Dunquin, takes 20 minutes, and costs €30. Try Blasket Island Boatmen (Tel: 066 915 6422; www.blasketisland.com) or Larry's Blasket Ferry (Tel: 087 743 5442). A 45-minute ferry also runs from Dingle town and costs €35 – contact Dingle Bay Charters for details (Tel: 087 672 6100; www.dinglebaycharters.com).

The cottages of the deserted village at the start and finish of the walk.

S ituated 2km off the tip of the Dingle Peninsula, the Blasket Islands are Ireland's most westerly land mass. The largest island, Great Blasket, measures 6km long by 1.2km wide, and was inhabited until 1953. Even at its peak, this small, Irish-speaking fishing community never included more than 175 people. The vast majority of the land is now owned by the state, which has proposed that the island be preserved as a national park.

The ruined stone buildings of the deserted village provide the first, poignant landmark of the route. From this evocative start, you climb up and around the mountainous spine of the island. Though the landscape is wild and remote, the terrain underfoot is relatively easy. Paths and tracks are followed throughout, and the route is suitable for most fit walkers. You also have a high chance of seeing various species of wildlife, including seals, rabbits, seabirds, basking sharks and dolphins. Overall, this is an immensely exhilarating and memorable route, which will remain etched on your mind long after you have finished.

To get the most out of your trip, it is worth combining the walk with a visit to the Blasket Centre in Dunquin, where you can learn more about

ROUTE 41:
Slieve Mish Circuit

This route over the highest peaks in the Slieve Mish range combines great views with the other-worldly atmosphere of Derrymore Glen.

Grade:	4
Time:	4½–5½ hours
Distance:	11km (7 miles)
Ascent:	900m (2,950ft)
Map:	OSi 1:50,000 sheet 71

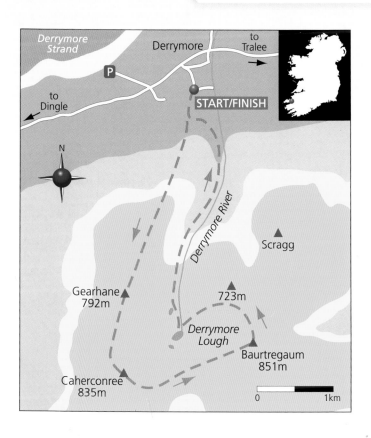

The wonderful views along the Dingle Peninsula from the Slieve Mish Mountains.

Start & Finish: The route starts and finishes at the end of a lane near Derrymore Bridge (grid reference: Q742106). From Tralee, follow the N86 southwest towards Dingle. After 10km, and around 500m west of Derrymore Bridge, turn left onto a minor road. Climb steeply for 400m and turn right at a T-junction. Park beside a small cottage at the end of the road, where there is space for about five cars.

This circuit visits the highest three peaks in Kerry's Slieve Mish Mountains, and provides a wonderful vantage point over the coast and mountains of the Dingle Peninsula. The highest summit of the route is Baurtregaum at 851m. This name derives from the Irish *Bár Trí gCúm*, meaning 'Top of the Three Hollows'. A fitting label given that Derrymore Glen, the amphitheatre at the heart of the horseshoe, is home to a string of three paternoster lakes. The glen is a wonderfully secluded and evocative place, and is visited on the return leg of the walk.

Despite its location close to Tralee, the route feels relatively remote, and there are no paths to guide you across the high ground. Fortunately, the well-defined ridgelines mean navigation is a relatively simple matter in clear conditions. However, the precipitous drops into the central glen mean you should exercise extreme caution in poor visibility.

The Walk

Begin by following a grass track that leads from the end of the road, past the cottage and round to the right. Just 100m later, turn left and cross a stile to reach the open commonage beneath the Slieve Mish Mountains.

On the path near the summit of Diamond Hill, with Kylemore Lough below.

Start & Finish: The route starts and finishes at the car park for Connemara National Park visitor centre (grid reference: L711573). Begin by heading to the village of Letterfrack, on the N59 Leenaun–Clifden road. A few hundred metres west of the village centre, turn south off the N59 and follow the signed access road up to the large parking area.

At 445m high, Diamond Hill should be a fairly modest summit, but in reality it has almost as much character as mountains that rise twice as high. A far-flung westerly satellite of the Twelve Bens, it rises in isolation above the village of Letterfrack, its steep slopes narrowing to a fin of quartzite some 500m long.

When Diamond Hill was incorporated into Connemara National Park it became an immediate hit, and for many people it served as their first taste of hillwalking in Ireland. The resulting erosion prompted the construction of a proper mountain path, which now allows even more visitors to appreciate the fantastic views across the surrounding peaks and coastline. The path is signed throughout but the ground remains mountainous on the upper slopes, and you may find yourself using your hands for assistance in some places. In wet weather the quartzite becomes slippery and care is needed.

The route is located entirely within the boundaries of Connemara National Park. It can be combined with a trip to the visitor centre, which is open between March and October and has exhibits detailing the history and ecology of the park.

The Walk

From the car park, walk past the old admission kiosk and descend along a gravel path to the visitor centre. Unless you want to detour inside to see the exhibits, continue past the entrance and around the north side of the building. Pass a children's play area, then follow a wide gravel path northeast, heading away from the whitewashed park buildings and climbing gently along the left side of a field.

The pyramid of Diamond Hill fills the scene ahead as you continue through a sprung gate and climb around an abrupt corner. The trail now heads back southeast to a junction. Turn left here, following the signs for the Lower Diamond Hill Walk. The path begins to climb gently now, crossing sections of wooden boardwalk where the ground is wet underfoot. Soon you reach a junction marked by a huge boulder. Turn left here onto the Upper Diamond Hill Walk.

After a relatively flat section, the gradient begins to increase as you approach the base of the summit slopes. Turn left at another trail junction, which you will return to during your descent. Now climb a flight of steep, winding flagstone steps. Fine views below allow you to appreciate the broken and intricate nature of the Connemara coastline, the maze of islands, bays, inlets and loughs so intricately interwoven that the division between land and ocean becomes blurred.

The path skirts beneath a steep slope, then climbs diagonally through a cluster of quartzite outcrops. A short distance later it emerges onto the upper part of the summit ridge, where the gradient eases. A final gentle climb brings you to the summit cairn, where you can enjoy sensational views across the Twelve Bens to the east. Below to the northeast is Kylemore Lough, with the Gothic turrets of Kylemore Abbey conspicuous on the lakeshore, while to the north, Connacht's highest summit, Mweelrea, peeps out from behind Doughruagh.

From the summit of Diamond Hill, many walkers seem to simply retrace their outward steps. This is a mistake, however, as continuing along the Upper Diamond Hill loop offers a more varied return. After an initially steep descent down the eastern flanks of the mountain, you can enjoy a largely flat return trip along the large terrace on its southern side. You may also get the chance to see the herd of feral goats that frequent the area.

Continue around the western side of the mountain until you return to the upper loop junction passed on your outward journey. Turn left here and descend to the junction marked by the boulder. Here you should turn left to complete the final part of the lower loop. Descend steeply to an old bog road in the Owengarve Valley, which leads you to a final junction. Turn right here to arrive back at the visitor centre.

ROUTE 33:
Glencorbet Horseshoe

This strenuous but scenic circuit includes several rocky ascents, and visits the highest summit in County Galway.

Grade:	5
Time:	6–7 hours
Distance:	14km (9 miles)
Ascent:	1,140m (3,740ft)
Map:	OSi 1:50,000 sheet 37, or Harvey Superwalker 1:30,000 *Connemara*.

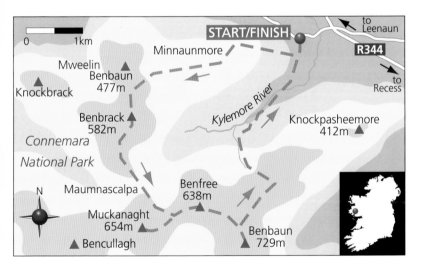

Start & Finish: The route starts and finishes at the end of a rough track at grid reference: L796574. Approach the area via the R344 Leenaun–Recess road, then turn west around 2km from the northern end of the road. Cross the Kylemore River, and park in a stony lay-by just past the track.

The Twelve Ben mountains are renowned as one of the most rugged and challenging ranges in Ireland. There are several fantastic circuits to choose from, almost all of which involve long hours and significant amounts of ascent. This scenic horseshoe route is no exception.

The high point is Benbaun, the highest peak in County Galway at 729m. This mountain lies at the very heart of the Twelve Bens, with all the main ridges of the range radiating out around it. The Irish name *Binn Bhán* translates as White Peak, which is a reference to the mass of white rock – mainly quartz – that covers its upper slopes. Benbrack, which is visited earlier in the day, is similarly shrouded in rock, while the middle peak, Muckanaght, is largely covered by grass. Muckanaght's slopes are very steep, however; there is a choice of two challenging ascent routes, or you may prefer to bypass this summit all together.

Note that the circuit includes two peaks with name Benbaun, so take care to avoid confusion. The terrain is complex enough that the route should be avoided in poor visibility, while the crossing of the Kylemore River will be awkward after heavy rain.

Walker surveying the route ahead from the ridge between
Minnaunmore and Benbaun (477m).

The Walk

Begin by following the track south for 500m. Just before the track starts to descend, turn right onto the open hillside. Climb gradually over the rough, rock-studded grass to reach the ridge top just west of Minnaumore. Cross carefully over a fence as you arrive at the ridge, where you are rewarded by a sudden view north over Kylemore Lough.

Now turn left and follow the ridge west. The shoulder is wide and rounded, and undulates across countless hummocks and several boggy patches. Descend slightly to a shallow col beneath Benbaun, then climb steadily climb up the rocky slope ahead to reach the ridge between Benbaun and Benbrack.

At the ridgeline you are met by another wonderful view. The nineteenth-century castle of Kylemore Abbey lies on the shore of Pollacappul Lough at the bottom of the valley, backed by the Garraun massif, the Connemara coastline and the island of Inishturk. Turn left onto a path that runs along the top of the ridge, following the trail up the rocky slope towards Benbrack. The climb is enjoyable, taking you over a couple of rock outcrops and past several more viewpoints before arriving at the summit cairn.

The descent begins in a southwesterly direction, then veers south across peaty ground to reach the col of Maumnascalpa. The col is marked by several peat hags, though these can be easily bypassed on either side. You now have a choice of routes. If you are not daunted by the precipitous slope ahead, it is just about possible to climb Muckanaght along its northern ridge. From the col, begin by climbing an obvious ramp between two low crags. You will need to take great care during the ascent because the steep grass can be slippery when wet, and there are several bands of rock to avoid along the way.

Faced with this precipitous ascent, most walkers prefer to climb diagonally southeast across the middle slopes of the mountain. A faint path through the grass will help direct you to the col beneath Benfree. From here you can either chose to bypass Muckanaght all together (saving yourself 180m ascent), or make an out-and-back approach along the mountain's eastern ridge. The ascent here is still steep, but definitely easier than the north ridge. The compact summit is marked by a cairn and fine views that include Killary Harbour.

Return to the col and continue east, where a short, steep ascent brings you to the small cairn at the summit of Benfree. Now descend southeast towards the scree-covered peak of Benbaun. As you re-enter the rocks, a stony path forms underfoot, leading you easily up the slope. At the top of the mountain, you pass first a large stone cairn, then, 100m later, the broken trig pillar. The incredible views encompass the rugged ridges of the southern Bens as well as the Maumturk Mountains to the east.

To descend, reverse your approach route past the large cairn. Roughly 100m later, another tiny cairn marks the top of the descent northeast. Pick your way carefully over scree and loose rocks to reach firmer ground below. Progress remains awkward almost all the way to the col, which holds a small lough on its right-hand side. Turn left here and descend northwest, following along the eastern bank of a stream. The grassy slope is steep in places but you can see your target: a tight cluster of grey-roofed buildings in the valley below.

Cross a fence beside the buildings, then join the end of a rough track. Turn right here and follow the track past several more buildings to the river bank. The old bridge has been washed away, so you will need to hop across the water at its shallowest point. Follow the track for the final kilometre back to the start.

The final climb along the northwest shoulder of Benbaun (729m).

Glencoaghan Horseshoe

A true classic that necessitates some scrambling across narrow ridges, this challenging route is a rite of passage for experienced hillwalkers.

Grade:	5
Time:	8–9 hours
Distance:	16km (10 miles)
Ascent:	1,500m (4,920ft)
Map:	OSi 1:50,000 sheets 37 and 44, or Harvey Superwalker 1:30,000 *Connemara*.

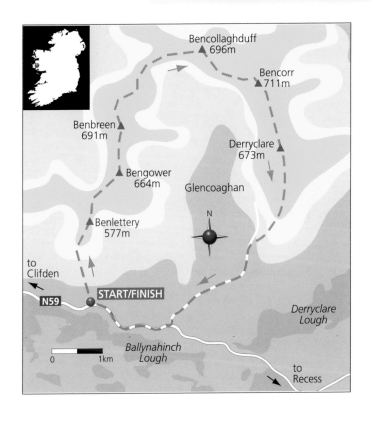

Start & Finish: The route starts and finishes at Ben Lettery Youth Hostel (grid reference: L777483). This situated on the northern side of the N59, about 13km east of Clifden and 9km west of Recess. Park along the old road beside the hostel entrance.

If you have a second car, leave it in one of several small lay-bys at the base of Derryclare's southern ridge (grid reference: L807493). To reach this point from the youth hostel, continue east along the N59 for 1.5km, then turn left onto a minor road signed for Canal Connemara Ponies.

Traversing six distinct peaks and with a total ascent of 1,500m, this circuit is a serious undertaking for even the most seasoned mountain walker. Nonetheless, the promise of exciting ridgeline scrambling and fine views over the wild Connemara landscape lures more hillwalkers to this route than any other in the Twelve Bens.

It does not take long to discover that the circuit's reputation is entirely justified. High ground on the route is, almost without exception, extremely steep and rocky, and in several places hands are required to help mount rock steps. Navigation is also a real challenge, and route finding can be particularly tricky if the cloud base is down below the summits. On the other hand, the stark beauty of the area is undeniable. There is no better vantage point from which to appreciate the south Connemara coastline than the barren ridges of the southern Bens.

This is essentially a circular walk, but if you do have two means of transport you can avoid walking the final 4km of road that links the two arms of the horseshoe.

The Walk

Pass through the gateway to Ben Lettery Youth Hostel and follow the drive towards the house. Just to the right of the building, beneath a large tree, you will find a protective plastic strip across a wire fence. Cross the fence here and climb the slope behind the hostel, crossing carefully over another wire fence after 200m. (This initial section is the only private land of the route; ask the farmer for permission if you see him nearby.)

The mountain of Benlettery now rises directly in front of you. The ascent is steep and steady from bottom to top, and a path is visible in places over the boggy ground. Rocks become more numerous as you climb, and near the top the path circles west up some wide gullies between the crags. The crown of the mountain is composed of boulders and slabs of rock, and this stark terrain will continue for most of the day. The summit is marked by a large cairn and the view is stunning; hundreds of interconnected loughs glisten in a 180° sweep below you, with the whole scene framed by the intricate coastline of south Connemara.

The view southeast from the summit of Benbreen.

Descend slightly east of north to reach a broad, peaty col, then swing east along the ridge, passing a subsidiary cairn as you climb towards Bengower (mislabelled Glengower on the OS map). In clear conditions, Bengower summit provides a great perspective over the horseshoe of peaks ahead of you. In bad weather, this is where the navigational problems really begin.

Head northwest from the summit cairn, following a rough path across loose stones. You soon arrive at what seems like a cliff of rock – the terrain from here to the col is the steepest (and most exciting!) of the circuit. Hands will certainly be called on to help lower yourself down over steps and slabs; follow the traces of those who have passed before and trust that there is a way to the bottom.

Cross the rocky col and immediately begin to climb again, heading up the steep scree-covered slope of Benbreen. It is possible to pick your way beside the scree initially, but there is no alternative to scrambling over the rocks to reach the cairn at the top. Dropping off Benbreen in the right place is perhaps the biggest navigational challenge of the circuit. The summit ridge, with its numerous rises and dips, swings northwest and then northeast in a semicircular arc. Continue right to the end of the arc before descending steeply down the wide rocky ridge to the col.

You are now at the apex of the horseshoe and truly in the heart of the Twelve Bens. The grassy slopes of Benbaun – the highest peak of the massif – rise just to the north. There is also an escape route south off the ridge down the Glencoaghan Valley, though the ground along the river is wet and heavy going.

To continue the circuit, skirt around the right-hand side of a crag at the bottom of the ascent to Bencollaghduff, then swing east up the rocky ridge. The ground evens out slightly and then becomes very steep and narrow just before the summit. Hands are called into use once more, but again a rough path will guide you between the outcrops to the compact summit. From here Mweelrea and the Sheeffry Hills come into view to the north.

Descend southeast over easier terrain, a welcome respite for strained calf muscles. The ground still consists of rocky pavement, but the slope is broad and gradual. Any relief is short-lived, however, because after a narrow band of peat in the dramatically named Devil's Col, the ground steepens once more. Large rocks and then ribbons of scree must be negotiated before you mount a rise and reach a subsidiary cairn. Take care to bear southwest along the ridge from this cairn, crossing several subsidiary rises before reaching the summit of Bencorr. The sprawling cairn marks the highest point of the circuit at 711m, with panoramic views encompassing Lough Inagh and the Maumturk Mountains to the east.

A steep descent brings you to a peaty col, then undulating terrain gives way to the final climb to Derryclare. Though this is the last peak of the circuit and the lane can already be seen in the valley below, avoid the temptation to rush off to the west after leaving the summit. Instead, follow the path along the crest of the southern ridge and veer west to join the lane only near the bottom of the slope.

If you are lucky, you may have left a vehicle along the lane near here. If not, turn left as you join the tarmac and continue for 2km to the junction with the N59. Turn right here and follow this road for 2km to return to your starting point.

The Central Maumturks – North

This fantastic route negotiates challenging terrain on a high, rocky ridge with magnificent views.

Grade:	4
Time:	5–6 hours
Distance:	14km (8½ miles)
Ascent:	810m (2,660ft)
Map:	OSi 1:50,000 sheets 37, or Harvey Superwalker 1:30,000 *Connemara*.

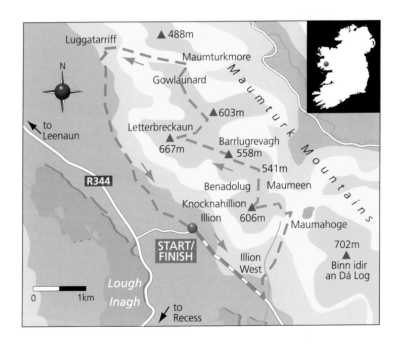

Enjoying the fabulous view towards Killary Harbour from the summit of Letterbreckaun.

Start & Finish: The route starts and finishes at the end of a track at grid reference: L859534. Access the area via the R344 Leenaun–Recess road. Just south of the Lough Inagh Lodge Hotel, look out for a turn to the east, signed to Maumeen. Just 1.5km later, you come to a sharp right-hand bend, with a track leading off to the left. The track is signed as the Western Way, and there is parking space for around four vehicles on the verge near the junction.

The Maumturk Mountains are amongst the most challenging mountain ranges in Ireland. They stretch for some 25km between Killary Harbour and Maam Cross. The northern summits are grassy and rounded, but as you reach the knotted ridge connecting the central peaks, quartzite takes over. The remainder of the range is dominated by cliffs, gullies, slabs, scree and just about every other rock obstacle you can imagine. Between these sinuous ridges there are several low passes, and these are the key to completing manageable circular walks.

The central part of the range, between Maumeen and Maumturkmore, is the rockiest and most challenging of all. Here we describe the northern part of that section, across Knocknahillion (606m) and Letterbreckaun (667m). These mountains are accessed via a short stretch along the Inagh Valley road, and a return walk along the Western Way. The adjacent, southern part of the range is described on p. 130.

Finally, a word of caution. The Maumturks pose particular risks to walkers; there is a great deal of steep and dangerous ground and the terrain underfoot is very unforgiving. There is little room for navigational error, and safe escape routes are limited. Unless you are particularly confident of your route-finding skills, keep these routes for good visibility.

The Walk

From the end of the track, begin by walking southeast along the road for roughly 2km. Just before a concrete bridge, turn left and follow the northern bank of the stream that drains down from Maumahoge. Cross to the opposite side of the stream when you can, and follow its southern bank up through the valley, passing over firm slopes of close-cropped grass. Several small waterfalls are encountered on the way, and the whole scene feels quite alpine.

The valley floor flattens briefly before you reach the headwall. You must now zigzag up this steep, grassy slope, using sheep tracks where you can find them. A sustained effort brings you out on Maumahoge where there is some welcome respite. However, rather than stopping immediately for a rest, you will find the views are much better if you turn northwest and climb across some rocky terraces to gain some height above the col. You should now be able to see the beautiful lough tucked away under the northeast face of Barrslievenaroy.

As you resume the climb towards Knocknahillion, you must start by negotiating a steep shoulder. An informal trail appears underfoot, which can be followed up to a broken band of cliffs. The trail leads off to the left here; do not follow it too far, instead scramble up through the cliffs and onto easier ground above. From this small terrace there are fantastic views back to Barrslievenaroy and across the Failmore Valley.

A final steep climb up increasingly rocky slopes brings you to Knocknahillion's summit cairn, which is set above a small terrace of tarns and boulders. The views now include the Twelve Bens and the rugged line of the 2km-long ridge linking Knocknahillion to Letterbreckaun.

The descent is rocky at first but gives way to easier ground at a peaty col. There is a possible escape route here that leads west, back to the road below. To continue along the ridge, follow an informal trail that contours southwest of point 541m. Next, pass the outlet of an unnamed lough before climbing past the shore of Loughaunnagrevagh. The ridge narrows and then steepens as you approach the boulder-strewn plateau of Letterbreckaun. The summit cairn is located towards the western side of the plateau, but views are somewhat restricted as the cairn is set back from the edge.

To reveal the views to the north fully, head east and pick your way over the boulders to descend onto Letterbreckaun's north ridge. Cross a small grassy hump, then pick your way down the rock ribs that cut across the ridge. The views are fantastic now, encompassing Mweelrea and the mouth of Killary Harbour.

Continue to descend steeply into Maumturkmore, keeping slightly east to avoid some crags. Once in the col, turn west and descend more gently down the valley. At the foot of the mountain turn left onto a track, and follow this south to join the Western Way. Continue south along this waymarked route, negotiating several boggy sections along this way. Keep to the left of a fence as you approach the junction with the road, where your vehicle should be waiting.

The Central Maumturks – South

Visit the highest peak in the Maumturks on this rocky but extremely scenic ridge-top traverse.

Grade: 4

Time: 5–6 hours

Distance: 13km (8 miles)

Ascent: 830m (2,720 ft)

Map: OSi 1:50,000 sheets 37 and 44, or Harve Superwalker 1:30,000 *Connemara*.

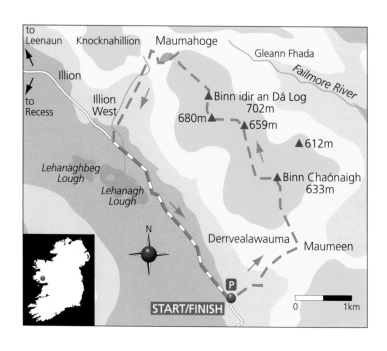

Start & Finish: The route starts and finishes at a large gravel car park beneath the col of Maumeen (grid reference: L892496). To reach the area from the south, leave the N59 at Caher, 2km east of Recess, and follow the signs to reach Maumeen some 3.5km later. From the north, take the R344 Leenaun–Recess road and look out for a turn signed to Maumeen just south of the Lough Inagh Lodge Hotel.

If you have two vehicles, you can avoid 3.5km of road walking by leaving a second vehicle on the verge beside a small concrete bridge at grid reference: L873521.

The Central Maumturks consist of a rugged quartzite ridge, whose peaks rear up in rocky, frost-shattered crowns. The route described here takes you across the highest point of the range, Binn Idir an Da Log at 702m. There is also a string of other rocky summits to negotiate along this characteristic snaking ridge, though the height loss between the peaks is relatively small.

Navigation is aided by an informal path that comes and goes along the ridge, while the Harvey map shows useful extra detail and labels several peaks that remain unnamed on the OS sheet. However, there is a great deal of dangerous ground on either side of the ridge and the consequences of making an error could be serious, so it is best to keep the route for clear conditions. Besides, the views are tremendous and it would be a shame to miss out on them.

The adjacent route across the northern part of the range is described on p. 127.

The view across Maumahoge during the descent from the main ridge.

The Walk

From the car park, follow an obvious stone track towards Maumeen. This climbs gently at first, then steepens as you wind through rock outcrops to reach the pass. Tradition has it that St Patrick blessed all of Connemara from here. The col still holds a statue of the saint, a tiny chapel and an outdoor altar topped with beautiful green Connemara marble. Stations of the Cross run around the site.

The ascent of Binn Chaonaigh starts directly behind the chapel. Climb to the left of a small cliff and continue steeply up grassy slopes. After a while you can use a fence, which is marked on the Harvey map, to guide you up the broad ridge. Follow the ridge as it swings north and leave the fence just south of Binn Chaonaigh. Now climb steeply to a lough, which you skirt around to reach the small cairn marking the rocky summit itself (633m). The views extend over most of southern Connemara, including the Twelve Bens to the west, and there is a good perspective along the ridge ahead to Binn Idir an Da Log.

Descend steeply across rock and scree, picking up a narrow path that leads down to a col at 523m. In poor conditions, the route's only escape route descends west from this col. The route itself continues north, following a clearer path that climbs steadily across rocky terrain then crosses a peaty terrace. Now weave through broken outcrops of rock to reach a small, unnamed summit. The ridge narrows here and the slopes on either side steepen precipitously, accentuating the feeling of elevation and further improving the tremendous views. Climb gently across broken ground, following the ridge around to the left. Pass a small cairn at 659m, then drop down to a gap on a lovely, narrow rock ridge. A steep climb now brings you to flatter, grassy terrain just south of Binn Idir an Da Log.

Continue across Binn Idir an Da Log and a small subsidiary summit, then begin the descent towards Maumahoge. In clear weather you will be able to see the descent route quite plainly, but in mist you will have to fight the tendency to follow the ridge into the Failmore Valley. Instead the route veers left and descends rugged slopes to reach the shore of a small lough. Pass around the western side of this lough. Now head northwest for a short distance, then southwest to locate a steep, grassy descent.

Once down on flatter ground you can relax and enjoy the atmospheric surroundings. Steep cliffs rise all around, contrasting with the gentle burble a stream to create a scene of almost alpine grandeur. Follow the stream down to the road. If you do not have transport waiting here, turn left onto the tarmac and walk the final 3.5km to return to Maumeen car park.

ROUTE 37:
Black Head

Exposed limestone pavement, several archaeological sites and fine coastal views all feature on this unusual circuit in the Burren.

Grade:	4
Time:	4½–5½ hours
Distance:	14.5km (9 miles)
Ascent:	410m (1,350ft)
Map:	OSi 1:50,000 sheet 51

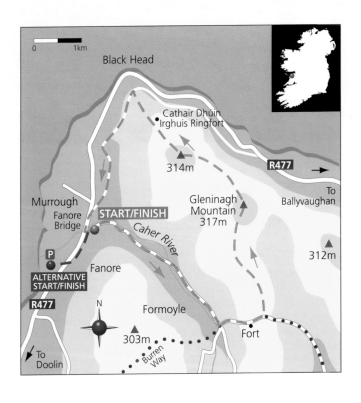

Start & Finish: The route starts and finishes in the village of Fanore, on the R477 coast road between Doolin and Ballyvaughan in County Clare. There is parking space for two cars outside the gates of St Patrick's church, which is signed 200m along the Khyber Pass road near the northern end of the village (grid reference: M147089). If these spaces are taken, use the large car park for Fanore Beach, 700m south along the R477 at grid reference: M140083.

The unique Burren landscape, looking south from Fanore.

The Burren is renowned for its unique geology, and the bare, terraced domes passed on this route are a classic example of the landscape of the region. The 340-million-year-old limestone pavement is broken every few inches by fissures known as clints and grikes, leaving an intriguing maze of rocky ledges for you to balance across. The cracks are often filled with wildflowers, creating miniature summer displays that will enthral casual and expert botanists alike.

The circuit includes an initial 3.5km section of road, but follows small tracks and open hillside for the remainder of the route. The 317m summit of Gleninagh Mountain provides the modest high point, and a second peak is crossed before you descend to one of the finest archaeological sites in the region: the Iron Age fort of Cathair Dhúin Irghuis. As well as the unique rock formations, fantastic coastal views are a feature throughout.

One word of caution: the rocky maze underfoot may be fascinating, but it is also potentially hazardous. Take care when placing your feet to avoid turning an ankle.

The Walk

If you park at Fanore Beach, add 1.8km to the total route distance. Begin by heading back to the R477 and turning left along the road. Take care of traffic as you walk 700m to the first right turn, signed for St Patrick's Church. After 200m you reach the church itself, and join the main circuit.

From St Patrick's Church, continue east along the road, which is known as the Khyber Pass and follows the line of the Caher River, the only surface river in the Burren. Climb steadily along the tarmac for 3.5km; traffic is light and the rapids to your left provide distraction. Eventually you reach a road junction, where waymarking posts indicate the route of the Burren Way. Continue ahead for another few metres, then turn left onto a winding stone track that is also signed as part of the Burren Way.

Climb along the track, past a collection of old farm buildings and the ruined fort of Cathair an Aird Rhois on the right. At the top of the hill, cross a stone wall on the left and strike out across open ground. The conspicuous green mound of Gleninagh Mountain is visible to the north, and the route veers northwest and then northeast along a rounded ridge to reach it. The ground underfoot is a mixture of grass and limestone pavement, and you will have to cross several stone walls along the way.

The summit of Gleninagh is marked by a trig pillar, and panoramic views encompass many of the hills of the Burren, as well as Galway Bay to the north. The next goal is the unnamed summit of 314m that lies to the northwest. Descend along a ridge to a col. Along the way you may find your way blocked by several short cliffs; skirt along the top of each obstacle until you find a point of weakness where you can descend more easily.

Once in the col, follow a wall that runs along its northeastern edge. The ground underfoot is almost exclusively limestone now. Climb northeast to reach the large cairn that marks the unnamed summit. This cairn is known as Dobhach Brainin. The coastal views are even better now, with the Aran Islands taking centre stage amid a wider panorama of Clare and Galway.

Descend northwest, skirting around several more cliff-like terraces. The circular stone walls of Cathair Dhúin Irghuis now come into sight ahead. This ring fort may once have been the seat of a Celtic king. It measures 25m in diameter by 4m high, and is one of around 400 ring forts across the Burren. Continue past the fort to reach an old green road, where a grassy track is enclosed by stone walls. Turn left and follow the track southwest towards Fanore, passing several more stone walls along the way.

Near the end of the green road you will find a jumble of rocks. Cross into the field on the left to avoid this obstacle. Now cross a final wall and join a gravel track, which leads to a junction with the R477. Turn left here and follow the tarmac for 400m to the Khyber Pass junction. If your car is at St Patrick's church, turn left here. Otherwise continue along the R477 for another 700m, then turn right to return to Fanore Beach car park.

Cliffs of Moher Coastal Path

This linear path passes above Ireland's most famous sea cliffs, with magnificent coastal scenery throughout.

Grade:	2
Time:	3½–4½ hours
Distance:	13km (8 miles)
Ascent:	240m (790ft)
Map:	OSi 1:50,000 sheets 51 and 57

Start & Finish: The route starts and finishes at a lay-by along the Killorglin–Glencar road, around 500m northeast of Lough Acoose (grid reference: V764864). There is also a larger car park just south of this lay-by, and several small, roadside parking spaces around the end of the Hydro Road, 1km north.

Carrauntoohil is a mountain that stands head and shoulders above any other in Ireland. Not only is it the country's highest point at 1,039m, it is also heavily fortified, with precipitous slopes and towering crags protecting it on all sides. There are several routes to the top, but none of them is easy and all require solid route finding skills and confidence over steep, rocky ground.

This route follows the classic Coomloughra Horseshoe, which offers 5km of fine, ridge-top walking above 800m high. The circuit includes the summits of Beenkeragh (1,010m), Carrauntoohil and Caher (1,001m), Ireland's second, first and third highest summits respectively. The crux of the route comes at a sharp, exposed arête that links Beenkeragh to Carrauntoohil. This ridge is notorious amongst Irish hillwalkers and you will need a cool head and favourable weather to cross it in safety.

A word of caution: the rocks along the ridge can become treacherous in wet or windy conditions. Also note that snow and ice can linger up here as late as April. Always be prepared to turn back if conditions are not on your side once you get to the ridge.

The Walk

From the lay-by, begin by heading northeast along the road. After 1km you reach the start of the Hydro Road on the right, marked by a mountain

Negotiating the rocky arête between Beenkeragh and Carrauntoohill in winter.

rescue information board. Pass through the gate and follow the concrete track for 2km, climbing steadily to the dam at the western end of Lough Eighter. There is now an impressive perspective of the ring of mighty peaks you are about to tackle.

Cross the lough's outlet stream and follow a path that climbs northeast towards Skregmore. The lower slopes are covered by heather, but this gives way to boulders and shattered slabs of rock as the slopes converge in a spiky crest. Follow the ridge over point 747m to reach the summit of Skregmore (848m). The already expansive views include Brandon Mountain at the tip of the Dingle Peninsula.

Head southeast along the ridge, crossing another unnamed summit at 851m. This brings you to the foot of a wide, rocky ridge beneath Beenkeragh. Follow a path up through the boulders and outcrops, perhaps using your hands for support in places. Ireland's second highest summit is marked by a small cairn, and heralded by sudden, spectacular views into the abyss of Hags Glen, and across a dizzying void to the cliffs on the north face of Carrauntoohil.

Amid all this exposure, it is no surprise that most walkers are slightly intimidated by the sight of the route's next obstacle: the ridge that links Beenkeragh to Carrauntoohil. This rock arête is just under 1km long, and has precipitous drops on both sides. If you proceed slowly and carefully, however, you will find there is really only one 30m section that is particularly exposed.

Begin by following a path that descends steeply just beneath the western crest of the shoulder. This brings you to the start of the ridge itself. Keep to the top of the arête until a sheer drop rears up on the left, and the trail moves to the right side of the ridge to avoid it. About halfway along you confront the rise at 959m. Follow the path back to the steeper left side to bypass this exposed rib, before returning to the right again.

As the ridge merges with broader slopes, a short, steep climb brings you to the top of Carrauntoohil. The summit is distinguished by a large metal cross and a circular stone shelter. New views extend east along the serrated ridge of the MacGillicuddy's Reeks, and south across the Black Valley.

Descend southwest from Carrauntoohil to a col, where the ridge narrows once more for the short, steep climb to the small cairn that marks the top of Caher. Continue west across a slightly lower summit at 975m, then begin the long descent home. After an initial rocky stretch the ground turns to peat, and a pleasant path leads down Caher's northwestern spur. Head for the western tip of Lough Eighter, where you can reverse your outward journey back to the start.

The Reeks Ridge

The apex of hillwalking in Ireland, this tremendous route takes you along the longest, most challenging ridgeline in the country.

Grade:	5
Time:	6–7 hours
Distance:	12km (7½ miles)
Ascent:	1100m (3,610ft)
Map:	OSi 1:50,000 sheet 78, OSi 1:25,000 *MacGillycuddy's Reeks*, or Harvey Superwalker 1:30,000 *MacGillycuddy's Reeks*.

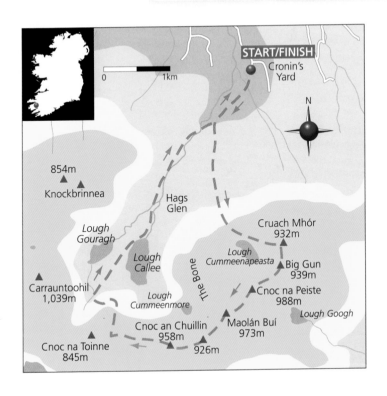

START/FINISH
Cronin's Yard

N

0 1km

854m
▲
Knockbrinnea

Hags Glen

Lough Gouragh

Lough Callee

Lough Cummeenapeasta

Cruach Mhór
932m

Big Gun
939m

The Bone

Lough Cummeenmore

▲
Carrauntoohil
1,039m

Cnoc na Peiste
988m

Lough Googh

▲
Cnoc an Chuillin
958m

Maolán Buí
973m

▲ 926m

▲
Cnoc na Toinne
845m

Start & Finish: The route starts and finishes at Cronin's Yard, at the end of the road in Hags Glen (grid reference: V836873). There is a €2 charge for using the car park here, and facilities include a tearoom, showers and toilets.

The MacGillycuddy's Reeks is Ireland's premier mountain range. It contains its eight highest peaks, as well as the most sustained stretch of ridgeline in the country. The route described here is the most challenging outing in this book, and includes 3km of exposed, sometimes knife-edge ridge over 900m high. The trip along this lofty arête is regarded as a rite of passage for ambitious mountain enthusiasts, and is only suitable for experienced walkers with a good head for heights.

The start at Cronin's Yard facilitates a relatively compact circuit, and enables a direct ascent onto the start of the ridge. The initial stretch between Cruach Mhór and Cnoc na Péiste is particularly exposed, and some confident scrambling manoeuvres are required here. Some groups chose to carry a short walking rope for extra security.

The Harvey map provides useful extra detail along the ridge, and also labels the main peaks, which remain unnamed on the OS map. It is best to avoid the route in high winds or poor visibility, and full mountaineering equipment is required in winter conditions.

If you are feeling especially energetic, it is also possible to extend this route west and complete a truly epic circuit that includes the two highest summits in Ireland. From the col at the head of Hags Glen, climb northwest to the summit of Carrauntoohil. Then head north along the ridge to Beenkeragh (see p. 148 for a full description). From Beenkeragh, descend northeast over Knockbrinnea (854m) to reach the Gaddagh River at the base of Hags Glen. This extension will add a further 2km and 440m of ascent to your day.

The Walk

Begin by passing through a metal gate at the top of Cronin's Yard. Follow a wide track along a field and past two more gates, and begin to climb gently above the Gaddagh River. After roughly 1km you arrive at a tributary stream, with a green metal bridge spanning the water ahead. Do not cross the bridge, but head upstream along eastern bank. Cross a metal stile after 200m, then climb southeast up the increasingly steep slope. Aim for the northern shore of Lough Cumeenapeasta, which offers good views west to Carrauntoohil and makes a natural spot for a rest.

When you are ready, head east from the lake and climb the steep rocks to reach the top of Cruach Mhór (932m). The summit is marked by a stone grotto, and provides your first view south across the Iveragh Peninsula.

Your main focus will be drawn closer to hand however, to the imposing, saw-toothed ridge that now heads south towards Big Gun (939m).

Progress along the ridge top is complicated at first by a some huge chunks of rock, and the best solution is to follow an intermittent path just to the right of the crest. Return to the top of the arête at a notch, then scramble carefully along the apex to reach the small cairn that marks Big Gun.

The ridge swings southwest now, and you can descend along the crest to a grassy col. As you begin the ascent to Cnoc na Peiste (988m) the shoulder narrows to a rocky knife-edge once again, but you can bypass the main difficulties using a path on the left. Rejoin the ridgeline just before the summit of the fourth highest mountain in Ireland. This is one of the most incredible viewpoints in the country, encompassing all of Ireland's mightiest peaks as well as the fearsome-looking ridge you have just traversed. High levels of adrenaline help to enhance your appreciation further.

The difficult terrain is now behind you, and you can stride south along a wide, stony ridge. Arc southwest as you descend to reach a grassy col, then make a short ascent to the 973m summit of Maolán Buí, the fifth tallest peak in Ireland.

Continue across an intermediary rise to Cnoc an Chuillin (958m), the final peak on the ridge. Now descend to a col and climb Cnoc na Toinne, a grassy rise with a long, flat top. About a third of the way along this plateau, at grid reference: V814835, look out on the right for a small pile of rocks that marks the top of the path known as the Zigzags. This grassy path descends through steep switchbacks on the northern side of the ridge, and deposits you near the base of the Devil's Ladder trail. Join this well-worn path and turn right, following it past the northwestern shore of Lough Callee. The track continues along the base of Hags Glen and returns to Cronin's Yard some 3km later.

Heading west along the awesome Reeks Ridge from Cnoc na Peiste.

ROUTE 44:
Coomasaharn

This impressive but little-visited route circumnavigates a series of cliff-bound, glacial corries.

Grade:	4
Time:	4½–5½ hours
Distance:	11.5km (7 miles)
Ascent:	800m (2,600ft)
Map:	OSi 1:50,000 sheet 78

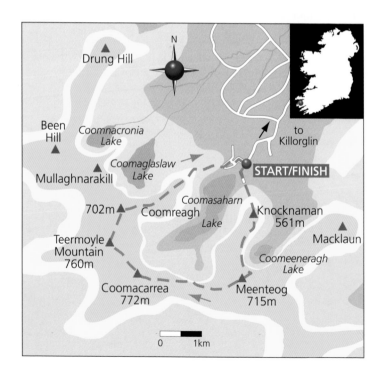

Start & Finish: The route starts and finishes near the end of a stone track at the northern tip of Coomasaharn (grid reference: V636852). To reach the area from Killorglin, take the N70 to the village of Glenbeigh and turn left up past the church. This narrow road climbs for several kilometres until you are almost on the shore of Coomasaharn Lake. The road turns sharply right here, and a track leads straight ahead. Park either beside a ruined stone building just before the bend or on grass verges near the end of the track, taking care not to impede access.

A hole in the mist allows a dramatic view along Coomasaharn from Teermoyle Mountain.

This wild route skirts around the top of high cliffs enclosing a series of deep, brooding corries. There are no fewer than six coums here, all of them gouged by the glaciers of the last ice age. Each coum contains a lake, ranging in size from Coomacullen Lake, a small pool ensconced within a high hanging valley, to the 2km-long Coumasaharn Lake that fills the floor of the largest corrie.

On its tour around the top of these steep basins, the route visits the summits of Meenteog (715m), Coomacarrea (772m) and Teermoyle Mountain (760m). The crux of the route comes during the descent from Teermoyle Mountain, where you cross a narrow ridge that is spectacularly exposed on both sides. As well as dramatic views into the corries themselves, the peaks also provide expansive panoramas north to the Dingle Peninsula and east to the MacGillycuddy's Reeks.

The steep cliffs and precipitous drops mean the circuit should be avoided in poor visibility and high winds. If you have two vehicles, it is also worth extending the route to include the western corries of Coomnacronia and Coomaglaslaw. From Teermoyle Mountain, head northwest across Mullaghnarakill, Been Hill and Drung Hill. Join the Kerry Way for the final 500m to the finish at grid reference: V620887.

The Walk

Begin by following the track southeast towards Coomasaharn Lake. Where the track dissipates, veer southeast and climb steeply towards Knocknaman. Negotiate a way through the rock outcrops to arrive at the top of the wide shoulder. You now have to cross the roughest terrain of the route, hopping across the marshy ground to reach Meenteog, some 1.5km southwest along the ridge. Keep to the eastern edge of the shoulder for the best views across the dramatic corrie holding Coomeeneragh Lake.

From the grassy, unmarked summit of Meenteog, fabulous views include most of the Iveragh Peninsula. Now turn sharply west and descend towards the col beneath Coomacarrea. Aim for the top of the sheer buttresses that protect beautiful Coomacullen Lake, where you can enjoy impressive views across the back walls of the corrie and down the length of Coomasaharn.

Follow an old wall and fence across the col, then begin the ascent to Coomacarrea. A steep climb up grassy slopes brings you to the iron cross that marks the windswept summit. Now descend northwest, following a line of old stakes to reach the broad col beneath Teermoyle Mountain. A short climb brings you to the top of this mountain. Either head northwest across the flat plateau to locate the summit cairn, or keep east and continue traversing along the top of the cliffs. The best views now lie to the north across Dingle Bay, with the long spit of sand at Inch particularly prominent.

Care must now be taken to ensure the correct line of descent along the Coomreagh ridge. Begin by heading north to point 702m. Descend east from here across a steep grassy slope with precipitous drops on both sides. The ridge narrows to a sharp, exposed arête for a short stretch and although progress is actually quite straightforward, the gaping holes of Coomaglaslaw to the north and Coomasaharn to the south ensure a thrilling finale to the circuit. A short climb marks the end of the difficulties and brings you to the broad summit of Coomreagh.

Descend easily northeast for around 1km. Where the shoulder narrows you should follow the ridgeline, keeping the rock outcrops to your left. As the slope broadens again, arc west towards the head of the Coomasaharn Lake. Join a rough track at the base of the slope and follow this to a paved road. Turn left here for 200m, then turn right onto a stony track. After another 200m you rejoin the road. Turn left for the final 500m back to the start of the route.

Gearhameen Horseshoe

A top-quality circuit around a beautifully wild valley, with superb views across to the MacGillycuddy's Reeks.

Grade:	4
Time:	4½–5½ hours
Distance:	10km (6 miles)
Ascent:	750m (2,460ft)
Map:	Maps: OSi 1:50,000 sheet 78, or Harvey Superwalker 1:30,000 *MacGillycuddy's Reeks*.

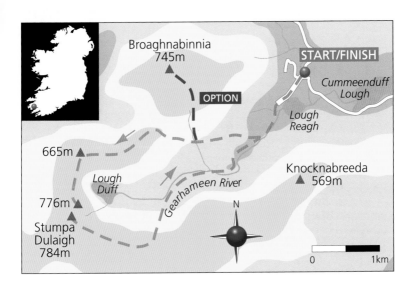

Looking across to the MacGillycuddy's Reeks from point 665m.

Start & Finish: The route starts and finishes at a small grassy lay-by, 1km west of Cummeenduff Lough at the head of the Black Valley (grid reference: V822813). The lay-by lies just north of a concrete bridge, and has space for around three vehicles.

The MacGillycuddy's Reeks are Ireland's highest and most impressive mountain range, and exercise a magnetic power over Irish hillwalkers. But sometimes their light shines so brightly it eclipses other routes nearby that would be considered exceptional if they were located outside of Kerry. The Gearhameen Horseshoe is one such route, and it holds such charm and scenic variety that it should not be missed.

The circuit takes you around a rugged and at times airy ridge that surrounds the source of the Gearhameen River. The main summit of the route, Stumpa Duloigh (784m), lies at the very head of the glen. There is some challenging terrain to be negotiated and dangerous slopes just off the route, so it is best completed in good visibility. The outing can also be extended by adding an ascent of the sloping pyramid of Broaghnabinnia (745m). This will add roughly 300m of vertical ascent and at least an extra hour to your trip.

The Walk

Walk south along the road and cross a small bridge spanning the Cummeenduff River. There is a metal gate almost immediately on your left. Pass through this and follow a track to a fork, where you should turn left and go through two gates in quick succession. Continue along the track, descending through woodland and rough meadows towards Lough Reagh. As you approach the lake the track begins to peter out, but a faint path can still be followed past the northwestern shore of the lake to an old stone sheep fold. About 50m from this pen you will see an ancient Ogham stone, with Ogham script still clearly visible along its left edge.

The Gearhameen River is conspicuous to the south, where it pours over a black crag. The descent route will provide a closer look at this waterfall, but for now you should strike southwest across open ground. Follow the line of least resistance to climb the rugged, rock-strewn slope between the Gearhameen River and a small tributary stream that descends from the southeastern slopes of Broaghnabinnia.

After roughly 200m of vertical ascent you reach a little prow of grassy ground with the river down to the left. If you want to add the extra ascent of Broaghnabinnia, head northwest here and make an out-and-back trip to the broad summit (a direct route from Broaghnabinnia to Stumpa Duloigh is rendered impossible by precipitous crags). To continue along the main circuit, climb diagonally west from the prow towards the northeastern shoulder of Stumpa Duloigh.

As you reach the shoulder you are greeted by an exhilarating surprise: an abrupt drop north into abyss of Coumreagh. Turn left now and climb steadily along the shoulder, with ever-expanding views all around. The view back north across Broaghnabinnia's mighty west face to the MacGillycuddy's Reeks is especially impressive.

As you gain height the ridge curves round to the south and becomes increasingly airy, with precipitous drops on both sides. Just beneath the summit you reach a rocky notch with an impressive view down a gully into the corrie holding Lough Duff. Do not attempt the direct ascent to the summit from this col as it is dangerous and exposed. Instead follow an obvious sheep track onto the steep slopes to the right, then climb diagonally towards the summit. Care is still required here, especially in icy conditions.

The summit of Stumpa Duloigh is rather non-descript, with no cairn and only a few small outcrops of rock breaking through the grass. The views are exceptional however, especially to the south where the entire Iveragh Peninsula is laid out before you.

Continue southeast across the flat summit ridge, then begin to descend the increasingly steep slopes using a fence as a navigational guide. Follow the fence down to a rugged saddle, then look for a steep, grassy tongue that drops to the left, passing through the crags on the northern side of the ridge. Descend with care, picking your way down onto easier ground high above the nascent Gearhameen River. Continue down to join this stream, then follow the river bank all the way down to Lough Reagh. Rejoin the old track at the northwestern corner of the lake and retrace your initial steps to the start.

ROUTE 46:
Torc Mountain

An ideal introduction to hillwalking, this out-and-back mountain path includes fabulous views and a 12m waterfall.

Grade:	3
Time:	3–4 hours
Distance:	8km (5 miles)
Ascent:	490m (1,610ft)
Map:	OSi 1:50,000 sheet 78, OSi 1:25,000 *Killarney National Park*, or Harvey Superwalker 1:30,000 *MacGillycuddy's Reeks*.

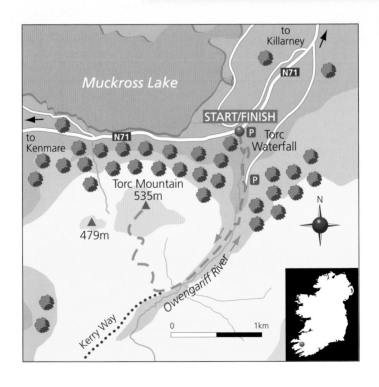

160

The view west over the MacGillycuddy's Reeks from the summit of Torc Mountain.

Start & Finish: The route starts and finishes at the main car park for Torc Waterfall (grid reference: V966847). This is located on the eastern side of the N71 Killarney–Kenmare road, around 6km south of Killarney.

Alternatively you could start at the upper car park (grid reference: V967842). From the N71, take a minor road south around 1.5km north of the main waterfall car park. Follow the road steeply uphill to reach the car park at the end of the road.

Torc Mountain in County Kerry is a modest hill that makes a big impression. Situated in the heart of Killarney National Park, the view from the 535m-high summit is the main attraction of the route. The outlook offers a magnificent panorama over the celebrated Killarney Lakes, backed by the peaks of Ireland's highest mountain chain. Other highlights include a mature native woodland, the celebrated 12m-high Torc Waterfall, and a section along the historic Old Kenmare Road.

Most Irish hillwalkers learn to associate viewpoints of this calibre with a significant amount of toil, yet the trip up Torc Mountain is not overly strenuous. There is no avoiding the 490m of ascent, and the mountainous nature of the route means you have to keep an eye on the weather. But the existence of a constructed mountain trail negates the need to contend with any rough terrain, and this is a walk that is suitable for almost all the family.

The route can also be shortened by 1.5km by starting at the upper car park. This will save you around 110m of ascent, but means you miss Torc Waterfall.

The Walk

From the main car park, follow signs to Torc Waterfall. A wide footpath leads through the woods to a viewpoint beneath the main falls, where the Owengarrif River plunges over a series of rocky walls on its way to Muckross Lake. The cascade is acclaimed as one of the finest waterfalls in Ireland, and is popular with tourists during the summer months.

From the base of the falls, turn left and begin to climb a flight of concrete steps. The path zigzags up the steep, wooded slope beside the waterfall, with handrails in place where necessary. The climb is sustained all the way to the top, and you rejoin the river just above its precipitous plunge.

This trail is also part of the Kerry Way, and you should follow signs for the 'Kerry Way to Kenmare' for the next kilometre. Turn left beside an old stone bridge and then, 20m later, turn right onto a sealed road. The upper car park that provides the alternative start/finish point is situated here on the opposite side of the road.

The road section lasts for just 100m before vehicle access is barred. Pass around the barrier and continue ahead along a track. The route now traces the old eighteenth-century Killarney–Kenmare road, the main thoroughfare between the two towns before the construction of the N71. In places the original cobblestones are still visible underfoot.

Follow the track over a bridge and turn left on the opposite bank, still walking through beautiful deciduous woodland. It is not long, however, before the trees fall back and you enter open, mountainous terrain beside a national park information board.

Continue to follow the track, climbing gently along the valley floor. Around 300m beyond the last trees, the path to Torc Mountain leads off to the right. It is now essentially a matter of following the path to the top. The route is clear as it winds gradually up the southern flanks of the mountain. Cut stones line part of the route, while boggier sections are crossed by wooden boardwalks wrapped with wire mesh for improved traction.

Less than an hour of climbing will bring you to the compact summit and its marvellous views. The town of Killarney lies below you to the north, and the Killarney Lakes are spread out to the north and southwest. Many of Kerry's most famous peaks are also visible, including the MacGillycuddy's Reeks directly to the west.

Once you have fully appreciated the view, retrace your steps down the mountain, past Torc Waterfall and back to the start.

Dursey Island

A cable car journey and fine ridge-top walking make this signed route a memorable experience.

Grade:	3
Time:	3½–4½ hours
Distance:	11.5km (7 miles)
Ascent:	410m (1,350ft)
Map:	OSi 1:50,000 sheet 84

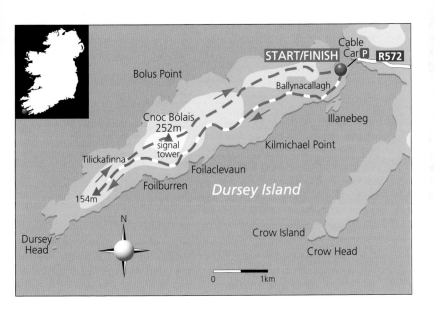

Start & Finish: The route starts and finishes at Dursey Island cable car station (grid reference: V505415). From Castletownbere, head west along the R572 for 22km, following signs for Dursey Island. Park in a large car park at the end of the road. The cable car operates daily except in high winds. From June to September it runs continuously from 9.30 a.m. to 8 p.m., and has scheduled service periods during the rest of the year. For the full timetable, see www.durseyisland.ie. The crossing takes about ten minutes and costs €8 return.

Dursey Island measures 6.5km long by 1.5km wide, and forms a hilly outpost at the tip of the Beara Peninsula. It is separated from the mainland by a channel 250m wide. This sound has a strong tidal race and is treacherous even in calm conditions. Fortunately, Ireland's only cable car offers an alternative means of transport, and the experience of swooping across the channel some 250m above the water provides a fitting introduction to an atmospheric island.

Dursey has been inhabited since the Bronze Age, though just six people remained by 2001. For walkers, the island's sometimes poignant history combines with an open ridgeline and stunning coastal scenery to make a memorable day out. The route described here is signed throughout, taking you along the old road to the western tip of the island, then climbing over the hilltops on the return. The off-road terrain consists mainly of short grass and heather, but boots are recommended for the occasional patch of bog and rock.

The Walk

The route is signed throughout with a mixture of purple and yellow arrows. From the cable car station, begin by following the single-track lane road that contours along the southern side of the island. The first landmark you pass is the stone ruin of St Mary's Abbey, an old monastery and graveyard near the shore around 350m south of the cable car. Just beyond this, the islet of Illanebeg was the site of an infamous massacre in 1602, when Queen Elizabeth's forces stormed a fort on the island and killed over 300 islanders, many of whom were simply thrown off the cliff.

After 1km you pass the hamlet of Ballynacallagh, the first of three, largely abandoned settlements on the island. The surrounding patchwork of stone-walled fields is testament to a more productive past. The second village, Kilmichael, comes less than a kilometre further on.

Keep left at a fork and continue along the road for another 3km, passing the third hamlet of Tilickafinna on the way. Where the road ends, continue ahead along a grassy track, climbing at least as far as the rise ahead. This 154m summit provides fine views over the western tip of Dursey, with its three attendant islets: The Cow, The Calf and Bull Rock.

Bull Rock, the northernmost island, holds a large sea arch, and was once believed to be a doorway to the otherworld.

It is possible to go all the way past point 97m to Dursey's western tip, but many people are happy to turn around at point 154m. From here, retrace your steps back to the end of the road. Now veer left, following a marked path up the ridge towards Cnoc Bólais, the highest point on the island.

Near the top of the slope, on the left, the remains of the word 'Eire' can be seen written in white stones on the ground. This was as a navigational marker for pilots during the Second World War. The 252m summit holds a remarkably intact signal tower dating from 1804, and incredible views in all directions. The panorama encompasses the Iveragh, Beara, Mizen and Sheep's Head peninsulas, and the jagged Skellig Islands to the northwest.

Descend east from the summit, crossing a stile and following a grassy track to a broad col. A gentle climb brings you over the next rise, then a steeper descent leads to a choice of routes in the saddle below.

To keep on the official route, veer right here, following signs for the cable car. A series of old tracks carries you around the fields and back to the road. Turn left along the road for 1km to return to the cable car station.

Alternatively you can continue along the ridge, climbing across open ground, past point 152m, to Knockaree. The ridge narrows enjoyably here, with a precipitous drop to the north and rocky outcrops underfoot. This option provides a wilder finale, prolonging the views and adding a bird's-eye perspective across Dursey Sound. From the summit of Knockaree, descend east along an informal path to return to the cable car station.

Descending towards Dursey Head, with The Calf (left), The Cow and Bull Rock (right) visible out to sea. Courtesy www.adrianhendroff.com

Cummeengeera Horseshoe

This rugged but immensely scenic route explores a ring of peaks around an imposing glacial corrie.

Grade:	4
Time:	4½–5½ hours
Distance:	11km (7 miles)
Ascent:	900m (2,950ft)
Map:	OSi 1:50,000 sheet 84

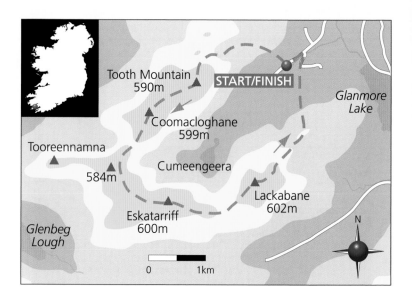

Start & Finish: The route starts and finishes along a lane at the base of the
Cummeengeera Valley (grid reference: V758558). Access the area from the
village of Lauragh. From here, follow the R571 west for 1km and look out for a
left turn signed for the Rabach Way. Around 1km later, turn right. Follow this
narrow road for 2km until it draws alongside the Drimminboy River. A track
leads left here, crossing an old concrete bridge with a gate in the middle.
The route crosses this bridge at the end of the circuit. Park along small grass
verges slightly further along the road, taking care not to impede access.

The horseshoe of peaks that encircle the Cummeengeera Valley form
probably the most scenic mountain walk on the Beara Peninsula.
The steep glacial corrie at the heart of the circuit is known either as
The Pocket or Rabach's Glen, in memory of a murderous outlaw who lived
and hid here in the early 1800s. The mountains loom over this remote vale
in a sometimes foreboding manner, and the second half of the walk in
particular features steep cliffs, narrow ridges and fabulous views.

The circuit carries you across the summits of Tooth Mountain (590m),
Coomacloghane (599m), Eskatarriff (600m) and Lackabane (602m). The
ground is rugged throughout, and you will spend a lot of time picking
your way over – or around – outcrops of sandstone rock. The route can be
followed in either direction, but you will need to take care with navigation
as the precipitous ground limits the number of safe ascent and descent
options. Try to avoid the route in poor visibility.

The Walk

Begin by heading southwest along the lane until you can see the
farmhouse at the end of the road. The Bronze Age site of Shronebirrane
Stone Circle lies within the garden of this house; if you want to get a closer
look, continue ahead and be prepared for the €4 entry charge. This route
turns right before you reach the house and begins to climb a broad spur
to the northwest.

Aim for a massive boulder that protrudes from the grassy slope above.
Hop carefully across a fence and pass beside the boulder, then begin
to climb more steeply. A line of rock buttresses blocks access above, so
veer left and begin to climb along the right-hand bank of the tumbling
Shronebirrane stream. You will need to negotiate some rough ground
before the gradient eases and you can pause to admire the already fine
view across the valley below.

The stream swings west now, and leads into a steep grass gully just
north of the imposing crags of Tooth Mountain. Follow the stream into the
gully, where a series of sheep tracks ease your ascent to the wide col above.

The saddle is transected by a fence; cross this, then follow it south, only leaving it for the final 100m climb to the rocky summit of Tooth Mountain.

Head southwest from this summit and descend to a rugged col, keeping to the southern side of the shoulder for the easiest progress and best views. An gradual climb then brings you to the trig point that marks the top of Coomacloghane. There are expansive views north from here across the Kenmare River to the Iveragh Peninsula, and a great perspective across the contorted sandstone crags that guard the head of Cummeengeera below.

Continue southwest, skirting to the left of some sharp crags as you descend. Another gradual ascent along a grassy shoulder brings you to flat ground at point 584m, then on to point 596m, which is marked by a small cairn. The slopes on the northern side of the ridge steepen precipitously now, and you head east along the cliff edge. Weave through a maze of rock outcrops and peat hags to reach the main summit of Eskatarriff, where more views open up south across wild Glanmore Valley to Hungry Hill.

The steep ascent to Tooth Mountain, with the Cummeengeera Valley below.

Looking across the Cummeengeera Valley from Tooth Mountain.

Progress remains awkward as you descend southeast towards the distinctive cone-shaped summit at 531m, which has impressive 200m-high cliffs cutting into its north face. Either climb this hummock or bypass it to the south, then make a steady ascent northeast across easier ground to reach Lackabane. This is the highest, and probably the most scenic summit of the route, and there are tremendous views in all directions.

Avoid the temptation to descend directly from Lackabane, heading northeast instead along an enjoyably airy ridge. Follow the spur across point 406m, then drop north and descend a steep, grassy slope, aiming for a green circle that indicates an old ring fort below. A short distance northeast of the fort, pass through a gate and join the end of a track. Turn left and follow the track for 500m, then cross the concrete bridge with the gate. Now turn left onto the road and walk the final few hundred metres back to the start.

Hungry Hill

This challenging but
immensely rewarding circuit
explores the most rugged and
complex mountain on the
Beara Peninsula.

Grade:	4
Time:	3½–4½ hours
Distance:	9km (5½ miles)
Ascent:	710m (2,330ft)
Map:	OSi 1:50,000 sheet 84

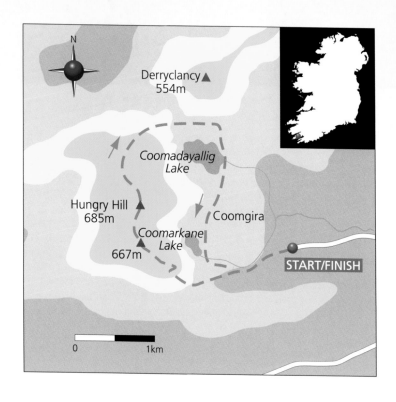

Start & Finish: The route starts and finishes at a lay-by at grid reference: V780493. Begin by heading to the village of Adrigole, on the southern side of the Beara Peninsula. From here, follow the R572 southwest for 1.5km. Pass over Reen Bridge, then turn immediately right. Follow this lane for 2km and park in a lay-by on the left, with a conspicuous wooden stile at the back. There is space here for several vehicles.

The mountains of the Beara Peninsula are renowned for their rugged character. Everywhere you look the sandstone skeleton of the peaks are laid bare in sweeping slabs, great terraced crags, and massive folds and whorls of bedrock. It makes for stunning scenery and equally challenging walking. Nowhere is this more pronounced than on Hungry Hill, a modest 685m-high summit topped by a thick blanket of bog but surrounded by impressive defences, especially on the eastern side where glacial action has carved out two huge corries.

This is the most popular route on Hungry Hill, but there are several other good options too. The southwest ridge is a more adventurous proposition and is normally considered an easy scrambling route, and you can also walk out and back from the Healy Pass. Whichever route you choose, this mountain is definitely not suited to conditions of poor visibility. There is so much dangerous ground, and the myriad cliffs and rock terraces make it difficult to follow a compass bearing. On a clear day, however, this is an immensely rewarding summit, providing superb views across much of west Cork and south Kerry.

The Walk

Cross the stile at the back of the lay-by and strike south across the slopes, making for the broken southeast shoulder of Hungry Hill. Already there are excellent views north across Coomgira, whose brooding crags fall abruptly to a valley floor patchworked with verdant fields. If there has been heavy rain in the previous few days, the Mare's Tail waterfall may also be conspicuous. This cascade, formed by one of the streams that drains into hidden Coomadayallig Lough, plunges through some 200 vertical metres and has a strong claim to being the highest waterfall in Ireland.

A climb of twenty to thirty minutes brings you onto the crest of the southeast shoulder. Now turn right and follow a fence west along the top, crossing a small stile and continuing over rough terrain to reach the base of Hungry Hill's intimidating southeast ridge. The route ahead weaves through slabs and small crags and is actually much easier than it looks. Follow the line of least resistance as you climb either directly through the middle of the obstacles or bypass them to the right. The key is to use the grassy ramps and terraces to zigzag around the larger crags. Near the top, a more substantial cliff can be passed on either side, though the easiest passage lies to the left. Beyond this the difficulties ease and a series of small stone cairns indicate the way to a larger cairn marking Hungry Hill's south summit (667m).

The views from here across the southern half of the Beara Peninsula – and in particular Bantry Bay and Bere Island – are especially good, and much better than from the actual summit. This lies just a few hundred metres north across flat, peaty ground and is distinguished by a trig pillar. Though the views to the south have now receded, this new vantage point allows a great outlook to the north and west, across the northern side of Beara to the peaks of the Iveragh Peninsula.

Leave the summit and head north, descending gently at first. As you reach the top of north shoulder, the gradient steepens and great ribs of sandstone erupt from the turf and run across your direction of travel. As on the ascent, you can use the ramps between these outcrops to zigzag your way down. Continue as far as the col beneath Derryclancy, where great views open up across Coomadayallig Lough. Contour around this lake, staying high on the southern slopes of Derryclancy before dropping down to the outlet stream. The immense sweeping slabs of sandstone that drop into the lough make this an impressive spot.

Cross the stream and climb south across a rugged spur. Now descend to Coomarkane Lake, another corrie lake surrounded by tremendous rock walls. Cross the outlet stream, then descend diagonally southeast before sweeping northeast and returning to the parking area.

The view northwards from the summit of Hungry Hill
(courtesy Adrian Hendroff: www.adrianhendroff.com)

ROUTE 50:
The Sheep's Head

Wild scenery and fantastic
coastal views lie at the tip of
this remote peninsula, which
offers signed paths with long
and short options.

Grade:	3
Time:	3½–4½ hours
Distance:	12.5km (8 miles)
Ascent:	320m (1,050ft)
Map:	OSi 1:50,000 sheet 88

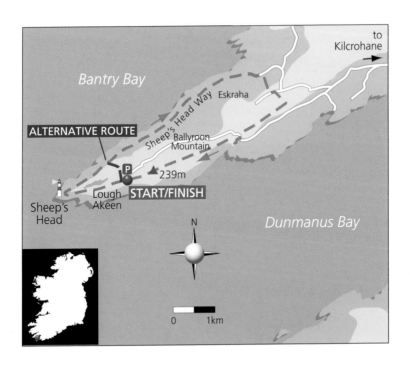

Start & Finish: The route starts and finishes at a car park at the western tip of the Sheep's Head Peninsula (grid reference: V733340). To access the area, follow the road along the southern side of the peninsula, passing through the village of Kilcrohane. From here, follow signs for 'Sheep's Head', continuing for a further 9km to reach the car park at the end of the road.

The Sheep's Head is the most isolated peninsula in southwest Ireland, and evokes a wild and rather primeval atmosphere. It is best summarised by the final line of Seamus Heaney's poem 'The Peninsula': 'Water and ground in their extremity'.

This walk explores the final few kilometres of land before the headland finally concedes to the sea. Most of the route follows the Sheep's Head Way, with stiles, signposts and footpaths in place to ease your progress. The terrain is generally undulating and the coastal views are wonderful throughout, with the summit of Ballyroon Mountain providing the modest highpoint at 239m.

The route described here is known as The Poet's Way, and is signed by red arrows. If you prefer a shorter walk, there is also a 4km loop that concentrates on the craggy terrain and lighthouse at the very tip of the headland. Follow the blue arrows to complete this shorter circuit.

The Walk

The long and short circuits follow the same route for the first 3km of the walk. From the car park, begin by heading west along the road for 50m,

The view across Lough Akeen, near the tip of the peninsula, with Bantry Bay behind.

then veer right onto a gravel footpath. This trail carries you easily across a delightful expanse of wild and rugged upland, then passes along the southern shore of scenic Lough Akeen.

At the end of the lake, cross a wooden footbridge, then climb to a helicopter landing pad encircled with white stones. Sheep's Head Lighthouse lies partway down the slope to the right of the helipad – you can access the building by descending a flight of concrete steps. The lighthouse is just 7m tall and was constructed in 1968 to mark the entrance of Bantry Bay.

Return to the helipad and turn left onto the path that runs along the northern side of the peninsula. There are several wet hollows here that you will either have to skirt around, or avoid by climbing a short distance up to the left. Pass along the top of some 100m-high cliffs, then climb gradually to a trail junction. The short route turns right here, weaving across rock-studded ground to return to the car park.

To stay on the longer route, keep straight ahead along the coast. Rocks become less frequent now, and you pass through swathes of thick grass. Descend past a pretty sea inlet decorated with a waterfall and a pair of rock arches, then continue over several grassy rises.

Soon the hamlet of Eskraha comes into sight ahead. Cross a stile and follow a track beneath the buildings. Turn left onto a minor road, then 100m later turn right over another stile and climb steeply alongside some fields.

This brings you to the spine of the peninsula, where you join a lane and follow it left for 50m. Now turn right, following another footpath across open, rugged terrain. Soon the trail turns right and begins to contour along the southern side of the hill, where you may have to skirt around the occasional wet patch. Negotiate several more stiles and continue past two small loughs before descending to a road.

Turn left along the tarmac for 20m, then turn right onto a lane. As you pass some houses the lane dwindles to a track, then shrinks to a footpath as you begin the ascent of Ballyroon Mountain. Climb along the apex of the ridge, with boulders and rock outcrops pushing through the grass below. The gradient is relatively benign, and fine views span both sides of the peninsula. As you near the summit, the first landmark is a pile of rocks that is actually a ruined signal tower dating from the early nineteenth century. The tower originally stood three storeys high and was intact until 1990, when it was blown down in a gale.

Continue ahead to reach the official summit, which is marked by a trig point and fabulous views both north and south across the Beara, Iveragh and Mizen Head peninsulas. The descent takes you past a square, concrete building, which was used as a lookout post during the Second World War. From here it is just a short distance back to the car park where the route began.

ROUTE 51:
Galtymore

A fantastic mountain circuit that includes tremendous views from Ireland's highest inland summit.

Grade:	5
Time:	5–6 hours
Distance:	12km (7½ miles)
Ascent:	1,020m (3,350ft)
Map:	OSi 1:50,000 sheet 74

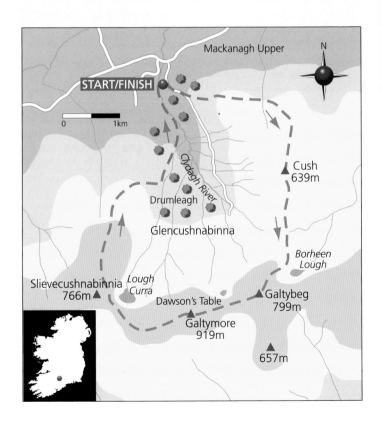

The Galtee Mountains rise above the fertile Glen of Aherlow.

Start & Finish: The route starts and finishes beside a forest entrance at grid reference: R 875278. Begin by heading to the village of Lisvarrinane in the Glen of Aherlow. From here, head east along the R663 for 1km, then turn right. A kilometre later, turn left at a T-junction. Continue for another 1km to a junction just east of Clydagh Bridge, then turn south onto a lane. Park at a forest entrance on the right around 300m further on.

The Galtees are Ireland's highest inland mountain range, their sandstone backbone formed of a line of rounded summits that extend some 20km across the patchwork farmland of County Tipperary. The peaks are connected by a high, meandering ridge with countless spurs and valleys fanning out on both sides. While the ridge's southern aspect is largely gentle and sloping, its northern flanks are precipitously steep and hold several deeply carved corries.

Galtymore is the highest summit in the range, and at 919m it is one of a select group of Irish peaks that qualify for Munro status. While there are straightforward approaches to the top via its benign southern slopes, the connoisseur's route is the circuit around Glencushnabinnia to the north. Not only does this include four distinct peaks, it also features the most dramatic mountain scenery in the area, focusing on the deep corries under Galtymore's northeast and northwest faces. Although navigation is relatively straightforward, the route includes several stretches along the top of high cliffs, so try not to walk in high winds or poor visibility.

The Walk

From the parking area, head uphill along the road for a few hundred metres. Look carefully here for a small path on the left, marked by a 'No Dogs Allowed' sign. Follow this path across a stile, then climb through thick heather to a second stile. Cross this and make your way onto the increasingly steep northwest shoulder of Cush. At 639m, this is a fine summit in its own right, and the trip along its elongated ridge is enjoyable, with superb views north towards Galtybeg and Galtymore and also south, back across the Glen of Aherlow.

Follow the remains of an old boundary wall as you descend south to a boggy col, then begin the long, steep ascent to the summit of Galtybeg (799m). The climb is not without its distractions, and there are particularly good views to the left, into the corrie holding Borheen Lough. The top of Galtybeg has no cairn but some small outcrops of rock lend it a bit of character. The views to the south are now revealed, and there is a particularly airy perspective over Lough Dineen, tucked away in the corrie beneath Galtymore's northeast face.

Now descend west towards the col beneath Galtymore. Unless the ground is very dry it is best to avoid the northern and central sections of this saddle, which can be a real quagmire. Aim instead for the southern side where the ground is a bit firmer. Then make your way back onto the ridge and begin the final big climb of the day to the top of Galtymore.

As befits the highest inland mountain in Ireland, the view from the summit is quite superb. On a clear day most of Munster is visible and you might even be able to pick out the outlines of mountains in Kerry and Wicklow. The summit itself is rather broad and flat, with a conspicuous white Celtic cross standing a short distance away from the official cairn.

Leave Galtymore in a westerly direction. The ground drops away gradually and soon you see the Galty Wall, an impressive land boundary that dates from the nineteenth century. This acts as a convenient handrail as the ridge swings northwest towards the dome of Slievecushnabinnia (766m). From here it is worth taking some time to appreciate the final great view of the route, back across Lough Curra to Galtymore itself.

Now make a gradual descent north along the broad shoulder of Knocknanuss, passing a prominent cairn. As the slopes on the right begin to ease, keep an eye out for a waymarking post set on a small hummock to the northeast. Aim for this, and join the route of the local Lough Curra walk. Follow the waymarks north to the boundary of Drumleagh Wood, then cross a stile and join a path along a wall. This brings you to a forest track. Turn left here and follow the signs along the track for a further 1.5km to return to the start.

Lough Muskry Circuit

This route combines a trip to an impressive glacial lake with a lofty traverse along the main Galtee ridge.

Grade:	4
Time:	4½–5½ hours
Distance:	13km (8 miles)
Ascent:	730m (2,400ft)
Map:	OSi 1:50,000 sheet 74

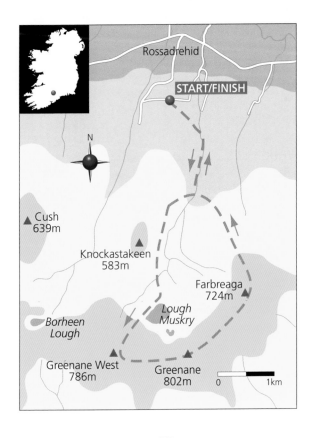

Start & Finish: The route starts and finishes at the end of a gravel road at grid reference: R917283. Begin by accessing the hamlet of Rossadrehid on the southern side of the Glen of Aherlow. From here, head south along a lane signed to Lake Muskry. After almost 1.5km, round a sharp right-hand bend then park 300m later on the left, where a double forest entrance encloses a small island of trees.

This route circumnavigates Lough Muskry, the largest glacial lake in the Galtee Mountains. The lough fills a hollow dammed by ancient moraine and is backed by sheer cliffs almost 300m high. It is a wild and atmospheric spot, and there are few signs that the lake is currently used as a source of drinking water for the surrounding communities. The upper part of the circuit continues across three high summits: Greenane West (786m), Greenane (802m) and Farbreaga (724m). Even here on the ridgeline there are signs of glacial topography; the conglomerate tor known as O'Loughnan's Castle is a former nunatak, sculpted by the freezing weather as it protruded from the surrounding ice sheet.

Reaching Lough Muskry is a fairly straightforward task, thanks to a track that leads directly to the lakeshore. The route is signed as far as here, and the 8km out-and-back trip to the lough is a popular excursion even if you do not intend to climb the mountains behind. Route finding across the scenic upland section remains relatively simple too, though the precipitous drop onto the corrie means it should be avoided in poor visibility or high winds.

The Walk

Begin by heading along the forest road, which quickly brings you to a junction. The waterworks building can be seen to the right here, but this route heads left, past a walk information board. From here to the lough you will be following the blue waymarking signs that mark the low-level Lake Muskry walk.

Keep left at a fork after 800m, then climb gradually through the trees. You arrive at the edge of the planation just over 1km later. Cross a stile beside a gate and take note of your location; you will need to re-enter the forest at this point during your descent.

For now, continue to follow the track as it climbs across open moorland on the western side of the valley. The track draws ever closer to the brooding corrie at the head of the glen, and brings you across a stream before arriving at the lake itself. The shore is a natural place to draw breath and admire the lough with its backdrop of imposing cliffs.

If you are continuing onto the surrounding peaks, this is where you must leave the waymarked route behind. Your aim now is the reach summit of Greenane West, which is marked on the map as point 786m. There is a

Walkers traversing the moraines above Lough Muskry (courtesy John G. O'Dywer).

choice of ascent routes depending on your liking for steep grassy slopes. The steepest, most direct option lies directly southwest from the end of the track, keeping well to the right of the cliffs. A less acute gradient can be found by returning along the track to the stream and following the bank of this watercourse uphill.

Whichever ascent route you choose, your arrival on the top of the ridge is greeted by sudden views that extend all the way to the south coast. Turn left here and walk east along the broad ridge, then descend to a wide, peaty col. Pass the fascinating rock tor of O'Loughnan's Castle, then climb easily along the top of the cliffs to reach the trig pillar at the summit of Greenane. More fine views include the remainder of the Galtee range, as well as the Comeragh and Knockmealdown Mountains to the southeast.

Turn northeast now and descend gradually towards Farbreaga. Part way along the spur you pass a cairn, which is dwarfed by the mass of stones sprawling from a ruined shelter at the summit of Farbreaga itself. To descend, continue northeast along the top of the shoulder for 200m, then veer northwest. Negotiate a way through a maze of contorted peat hags, then drop more easily to the valley floor. Cross the stream that flows along the base of the glen just above a wood, then climb back to the track. Turn right here and cross the stile at the forest boundary, then reverse your outward journey through the trees and back to the start.

Knockmealdown Circuit

Two routes explore the highest summit in the Knockmealdown Mountains: choose between a compact circuit or a long traverse that encompasses all the main peaks in the range.

Short Circuit

Grade:	4
Time:	4–5 hours
Distance:	11km (7 miles)
Ascent:	830m (2,720ft)
Map:	OSi 1:50,000 sheet 74

Long Traverse

Grade:	4
Time:	6½–7½ hours
Distance:	20.5km (12½ miles)
Ascent:	1,200m (3,940ft)
Map:	OSi 1:50,000 sheet 74

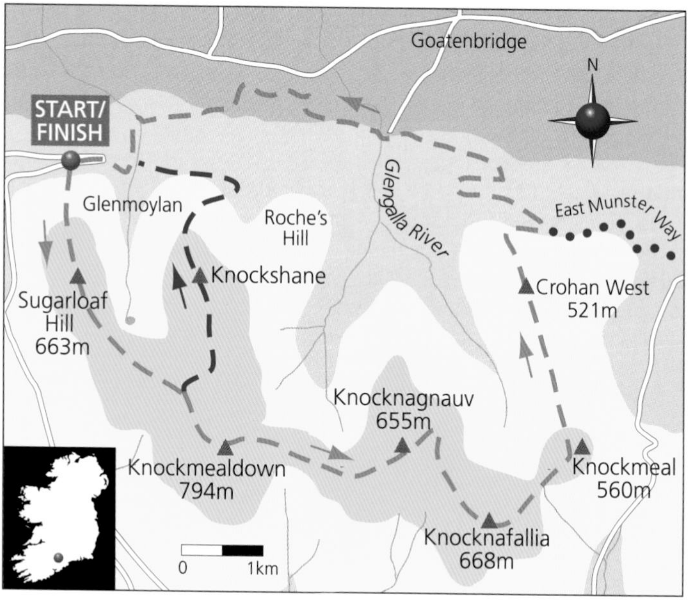

Start & Finish: The long and short routes both start and finish at a large roadside parking area just uphill from the switchback known as The Vee (grid reference: S041118), located along the R668 Clogheen–Lismore road, around 6km south of Clogheen.

If you want to complete the longer traverse and have two vehicles, you can save yourself 9km of walking by parking a second car along the Newcastle–Mellary road at grid reference: S041118. There is space here for around five cars.

The Knockmealdown Mountains are 25km long and span the border of counties Tipperary and Waterford. They contain at least fifteen distinct peaks, and rise to 794m at the summit of Knockmealdown itself. As well as being the highest point of the range, this mountain is also the most interesting topographically, and features the only glacial corrie in the area on its eastern flanks.

In this description we offer a choice of two mountain circuits. The long route is a traverse of the five main peaks in the eastern half of the range, and is one of the classic walks of the region. If you have two vehicles you can complete the upland part of this route only, otherwise a signed return along the East Munster Way brings you along forest tracks and back to the start.

The shorter alternative follows the same route to the summit of Knockmealdown, then diverts north along the shoulder of Knockshane. Both routes follow clear paths across much of the high ground, with the stone wall that marks the county border providing a useful navigational handrail.

The Walk

From the lay-by, cross the road and look for the start of a well-trodden trail. This climbs uphill, past a beehive-shaped monument that commemorates the local property owner Samuel Grubb. The ascent is sustained and the path is eroded in places, but it deposits you efficiently at the wide, cairn-strewn summit of Sugarloaf Hill (663m). Extensive views encompass the Comeragh and Galtee Mountains, as well as the vast patchwork of fields around the Suir Valley.

Now head southeast, following an obvious path beside the stone wall that acts as the country boundary. An easy descent and subsequent climb brings you to Knockmealdown's summit ridge, where you veer south and pass around the back of the mountain's eastern corrie (care is needed here in poor visibility). The trig pillar lies on the southern rim of the corrie, and provides more tremendous views that include Dungarvan Harbour and the River Blackwater to the south.

This is where you must decide if you want to complete the short or the long circuit. For the short loop, retrace your steps northwest along the

The view from Knocknafallia towards Knockmeal (courtesy John G. O'Dwyer).

summit ridge. Where the county wall drops left, veer northeast toward the rounded hump of Knockmoylan, which is marked as point 768m on the map. From the summit cairn, descend north along the broad, heathery spur of Knockshane, passing another cairn along the way. As the ground steepens, keep to the left side of the shoulder until you see an obvious path running alongside a forest fence below. Turn right onto this and follow it into the trees to a large turning circle. (Note that the OS map does not show the forest tracks correctly in this area.) Here you join a forest road, which descends though a wide switchback then passes two minor junctions, to reach a major fork. Keep right here, and at the next right bend, look out for a footpath on the left signed as part of the East Munster Way. Follow the waymarks across a footbridge over the Glenmoylan River, then leave the marked trail and turn left onto a path that climbs steeply back to The Vee.

For the longer circuit, descend steeply east from Knockmealdown summit. Pass through a broad col, then follow the path on a steady ascent to the twin peaks of Knocknagauv (655m), both of which are crowned by a cairn. The wall heads northeast here, then contours around the northern slopes of Knocknafallia. It is a shame to miss out on this peak however, so descend southeast from Knocknagauv to a wide col, then climb to the cairn that marks the 668m summit. The eastern side of the summit plateau also holds an ancient burial mound, which has unfortunately been disturbed to support a now ruined, modern shed.

Now descend northeast to reach the col beneath Knockmeal. In the saddle you meet a forest road and the path splits in three. Take the left-hand trail, then 50m later at a bend, turn up the slope and follow a faint path to the broad plateau. The small summit cairn lies about 80m east of the path.

If you have left a second vehicle along the Newcastle–Mellary road, descend directly east from Knockmeal to find your vehicle. Otherwise, begin a longer descent north along a narrow path. A rough climb brings you to the final summit of the route, Crohan West (521m), which is topped by a large cairn.

Descend directly north towards the forest, following a line of old posts until you reach a new fence marking the forest boundary. Head 20m left, then turn north again, following a path between a patch of mature forest and a large clear-felled area. This brings you to a track that is signed as part of the East Munster Way. The 18m round tower that honours Liam Lynch, leader of the IRA during the Irish Civil War, is a five-minute detour along this track to the right.

The main circuit turns left onto the track, and follows the signs for the East Munster Way for the next 8km. After roughly 3.5km, the Tipperary Heritage Way joins the route. Continue across a bridge over the Glengalla River, still following the track as it alternates between mature plantations and patches of clear-fell. Another 4km later, the route turns south, then brings you to a left-hand bend. At the apex of this bend, look out for a footpath on the right. Cross a footbridge over the Glenmoylan River, then leave the marked trail and turn left onto a path that winds steeply uphill and returns you to the road at The Vee.

Nire Valley Coums

This route explores five
dramatic corries on the
edge of the Comeragh
plateau, with fabulous
scenery throughout.

Grade:	4
Time:	5–6 hours
Distance:	15.5km (9½ miles)
Ascent:	800m (2,620ft)
Map:	OSi 1:50,000 sheet 75

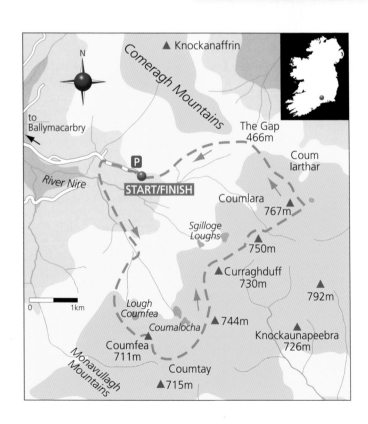

Start & Finish: The route starts and finishes at a large car park at the end of the road in the Nire Valley (grid reference: S276128). Begin by using the R671 Clonmel–Dungarvan road to reach the village of Ballymacarbry. Turn east here opposite Melody's Nire View bar and head along the Nire Valley Scenic Drive. At a junction roughly 5km later, keep right and follow this road for 4km to reach the car park at its end.

The Comeragh Mountains in County Waterford are home to some of the most spectacular examples of post-glacial landscaping in Ireland. No fewer than ten corries – or coums – cut into the margins of the massif, giving the range its name. Many of these corries also face west, an orientation that is unusual in Ireland.

This route makes a circuit around five coums on the north and western side of the sprawling Comeragh plateau. Each coum is appreciated from above, providing a bird's-eye perspective across the steep surrounding cliffs and the loughs that fill their base. The most impressive amphitheatre is probably Coum Iarthar, the final landmark of the route, and it is encouraging to have such a spectacular piece of natural architecture beckoning you on.

The corries are linked by short hops across the edge of the plateau, where the ground is surprisingly dry and peat-free. The only rough terrain comes on the final descent from Coum Iarthar back to the car park. Overall you spend roughly half the route tracing the top of precipitous drops, so try to avoid walking in poor visibility or high winds.

The Walk

From the parking area, begin by heading northwest back along the access road for roughly 500m. Turn left here, passing through a gate and descending along a track to reach the banks of the River Nire. Cross the bridge and continue straight ahead to a gate, beyond which lies open, mountainous terrain.

Now climb southeast along the northern bank of the stream that drains the twin coums above. After 1km the stream splits, with one branch heading towards Coumfea and the other towards Coumalocha. Turn southwest here, crossing both streams and climbing onto the broad spur that forms the western wall of Coumfea. A steady ascent south brings you to the top of this corrie; keep to the eastern side of the ridge for the best views across the tiered cliffs to the loughs below.

Follow the cliff line to point 711m, then follow a path that arcs around the rim of Coumalocha. Progress here is surprisingly easy, with firm grass underfoot, and the drama beneath your feet is complimented by long-distance views along the Nire Valley to the Galtee and Knockmealdown Mountains.

As the cliffs begin to ease at the northwestern edge of Coumalocha, contour north across slightly rougher terrain. A kilometre later you reach the top of the cliffs overlooking the Sgilloge Loughs, and can enjoy a new perspective across this smaller, but no less impressive coum. Follow the cliff line east, then cross a stream just above its abrupt plunge into the corrie below. A series of clear sheep trails now leads north, traversing a steep spur to reach a viewpoint above Coumlara. This slender coum lacks a lake but is bisected instead by a delicate waterfall.

Follow the lip of this corrie southeast, climbing above broken cliffs. Now swing northeast and cross the upper reaches of the stream that drains onto the coum. Head northeast from here, climbing towards the eastern end of the plateau surrounding point 767m. In less than 1km your progress will be suddenly halted by your arrival at Coum Iarthar, the final and most spectacular corrie of the route. This terraced coum holds a series of four paternoster lakes, while the surrounding cliffs are broken into contorted free-standing formations.

Head northwest around the rim of Coum Iarthar, then descend the spur that drops down towards The Gap. Along the way you will need to skirt around the left side of some precipitous crags and weave through a maze of conglomerate boulders. Now follow a fence along the right side of the ridge, enjoying a fine view ahead across the Knockanaffrin Ridge.

At The Gap, turn left onto an old track marked with white posts. Part way down the slope the ground becomes wet and the trail dissipates somewhat, but it soon consolidates again as you continue to lose height. Soon the Nire Valley car park comes into sight below. Bear right now and a follow narrow path through the heather to the end.

Walking along the Nire Valley road at the start of the circuit.

Coumshingaun Circuit

This classic route involves some rocky scrambling and challenging terrain on its circumnavigation of perhaps the most spectacular corrie in Ireland.

Grade:	5
Time:	3½–4 hours
Distance:	8km (5 miles)
Ascent:	650m (2,130ft)
Map:	OSi 1:50,000 sheet 75

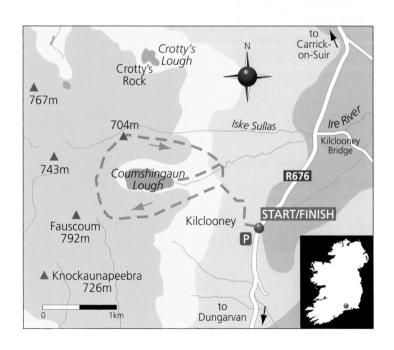

Start & Finish: The route starts and finishes at a car park in Kilclooney Forest (grid reference: S342102). Approach the area via the R676 Carrick-on-Suir to Dungarvan road. Turn west off this road at a sign for Kilclooney Forest to find the large parking area.

The view over Coumshingaun from the southwestern rim of the corrie.

Even set amid a range famed for its deep corries, Coumshingaun stands out. A precipitous amphitheatre hollowed from the rock by a lingering pocket of ice, this spectacular basin is often called the finest example of a glacial corrie in Ireland. Its headwall is almost 400m high and virtually sheer, while the lowering arms of the basin squeeze oppressively inward on either side. Deep within the pit, water has been constrained by an old moraine, creating a 700m-long lake that local myth will tell you is bottomless.

This route is one of the classics of southeast Ireland, and relatively simple in form. It makes a clean circuit of the corrie, with one brief, optional detour to visit the highest point of the range. The reality on the ground is rather different, however, and the terrain covered is anything but straightforward. The ascent along the southern edge of the corrie is particularly steep, and necessitates some easy scrambling manoeuvres as well as a cool head across steep, grassy slopes set above exposed drops. Predictably, the route is best avoided in poor visibility, strong winds and wet or icy conditions.

If you lack the experience to tackle the full circuit but still want to appreciate this majestic natural landmark, consider following the route described as far as the lough shore, then retrace your steps back to the car park.

The Walk

Begin by following a well-trodden path that starts in the northwest corner of the car park. The trail passes beneath dense trees and brings you to a forest road after 500m. Turn right here and climb gently along the road, past a communications mast disguised as a fake tree. Continue beneath some low-hanging boughs to reach a wire fence. Cross this with the help of a stile, then turn uphill along a rocky path.

When the trail veers west, cross the adjacent stone wall and climb towards the top of the ridge ahead. The crest marks the junction of the two arms of the circuit. To visit the shore of Coumshingaun Lough, descend to the lake from here. To stay on the longer route, turn left and follow the path along the crest of ridge.

Large outcrops of rock soon begin to litter the slope, and the path weaves a way through the obstacles. You will find yourself engaging in some enjoyable scrambling manoeuvres as you squeeze over and between the crags, and some trial and error may be necessary to locate the best route through the maze.

As the outcrops diminish, the ridge narrows and a steep, grassy spur continues skyward. There is now a precipitous drop to the north, and the path takes to the southern side of the ridge before rejoining the crest for the most challenging section of the route. Slowly and carefully, work your way up 50m of high, muddy steps, studiously ignoring the gaping exposure on both sides.

The tricky terrain is all behind you as you ease onto the flat ground of the Comeragh Plateau. After appreciating your lofty vantage point high above the amphitheatre, follow the cliff edge west along the top of the corrie. If you want to include a visit to the highest point of the Comeraghs, detour 500m west from the southwestern corner of the coum. An out-and-back trip across the peaty plateau will bring you to 792m Fauscoum, which is unnamed on the OS map, but marked on the ground by a cairn and and long-range views west to the Galtee and Knockmealdown Mountains.

Return to the corrie and head north along its western rim, where there are particularly dramatic views down the 380m-high cliffs at your feet. Continue around the northwestern coner and pass over point 704m. Keep to the crest of the ridge as you descend east, resisting the temptation to veer south too early to avoid steep crags below.

You will have to clamber through another band of rock outcrops before the gradient eases and you arc south, soon reaching a path heading towards the lake. If you like the idea of relaxing a while on the lough shore, turn right at this junction. Otherwise, keep straight ahead and climb to the base of the south ridge. From here you can retrace you initial steps back to the forest and car park.

Howth Cliff Path

A signed path carries you
past the dramatic cliffs and
surprisingly wild coastline of
the Howth Peninsula, just a
stone's throw from Dublin city.

Grade:	2
Time:	3–3½ hours
Distance:	10km (6 miles)
Ascent:	240m (790ft)
Map:	OSi 1:50,000 sheet 50

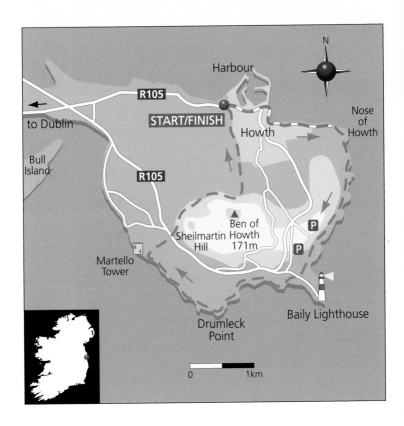

Start & Finish: The route starts and finishes at Howth DART station (grid reference: O282394). There are regular DART services from here to central Dublin and Greystones. If you are arriving by car, park in a large car park between the DART station and the harbour.

Though the coastline around much of Dublin Bay is predictably urban, it is enclosed to the north and south by headlands that are surprisingly wild in character. The peninsula of Howth, on the northern side of the city, boasts a 3km-long cliff line whose rugged and untamed nature would seem more at home on Ireland's western seaboard than alongside the country's largest metropolis.

The charms of the area are not lost on local inhabitants, who have long appreciated the escapism of strolling along their local cliff path. In recent years the headland's trails have been organised into a series of looped walks, and this route follows the longest trail. Known as the Bog of Frogs Loop, the circuit is signed throughout by purple arrows. Landmarks along the way include the Baily Lighthouse, and there is an optional detour to the summit of the 171m-high Ben of Howth.

Stiles and steps are in place wherever necessary, but much of the path remains distinctly wild so boots are definitely required. Note too that some sections of the trail pass along the top of steep cliffs, so you should avoid walking in strong winds.

The Walk

From Howth DART station, turn east and follow the purple arrows along the pavement. Cross a road and join a wide promenade that leads pleasantly around the back of the harbour and marina. When the promenade ends,

Following the path towards the Baily Lighthouse, at the southeastern tip of the Howth Peninsula.

bear right and follow Balscadden Road around the coast. The road climbs gently past Balscadden House, home to the poet W. B. Yeats between 1880 and 1883.

The tarmac comes to an end at a car park, and the cliff path continues ahead. The trail is obvious underfoot as it makes its way around the rough coastal slope. Already there is a good sense of wilderness in your surroundings, with fine views extending north over Lambay Island and the precipitous outcrop of Ireland's Eye.

Pass around the Nose of Howth, where the path sweeps south. You can now settle back and enjoy 2.5km of fine, uninterrupted coastal walking. Soon the Baily Lighthouse comes into view ahead, perched at the end of a promontory on the southeastern tip of the peninsula. At a path junction continue straight ahead, still following the purple arrows. A gradual descent now brings you to the lighthouse access road. There has been a lighthouse here since the mid 1600s but the present structure was built in 1814.

Cross straight over the road. The trail traces the southern coast of the peninsula for the next 3km, running along the top of low cliffs beneath a series of houses. The best views are now southward, across Dublin Bay to the Wicklow Mountains. Once you have passed Drumleck Point the trail descends to the shore itself, climbing up and down across a series of rocky coves. The next challenge is a flight of steps that have been cut into the rock, with handholds in place for safety.

A Martello Tower now comes into sight ahead. Continue to a path junction around 250m east of the tower, then turn right. Climb inland to a grassy meadow, where you should follow the signs left, then right. This brings you to a road, which you cross straight over.

Now climb across the eastern slopes of Sheilmartin Hill, following a trail bordered by bracken and gorse. This brings you to Howth Golf Course, where a line of white rocks guides you across the fairways. Continue across a small peat bog to reach the open shoulder of the Ben of Howth, and a path junction. Here you meet the red route, which descends from the masts to the right. A short detour along this trail will bring you to the 171m-high summit of the Ben of Howth, which provides good 360° views, though the foreground is blighted by three communication masts.

Back on the purple route, turn left at the trail junction and descend past deciduous woodland then the local GAA club. You arrive back in civilisation at the end of a suburban street. Follow the markers around a housing estate, keeping generally left at junctions. Now follow a paved pathway through a tunnel of trees – this is the route of an old tramway. The tramway deposits you neatly opposite Howth DART station, back where the circuit began.

Great Sugar Loaf

This iconic little peak features a short but steep ascent that is guaranteed to raise a smile from the whole family.

Out-and-Back from the South

Grade:	3
Time:	1–1¼ hours
Distance:	3km (2 miles)
Ascent:	210m (690ft)
Map:	OSi 1:50,000 sheet 56, or EastWest Mapping 1:30,000 *Wicklow East*.

Circuit from the East

Grade:	3
Time:	2–2½ hours
Distance:	5km (3 miles)
Ascent:	380m (1,250ft)
Map:	OSi 1:50,000 sheet 56, or EastWest Mapping 1:30,000 *Wicklow East*.

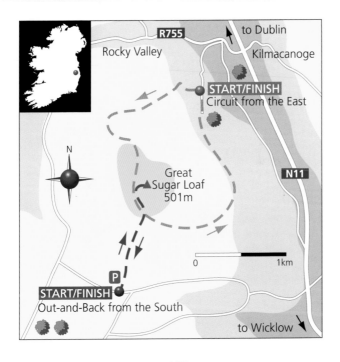

Despite its modest height of 501m, Great Sugar Loaf is one of Wicklow's most recognisable peaks. Its conical profile lends it a distinctly volcanic character, and it stands in sharp contrast to the more rolling contours of many of the other Wicklow mountains. Its position distinguishes it further: standing slightly aloof from the rest of the range, this natural landmark provides a familiar focal point from countless surrounding locations.

Despite its status as an icon of the region, this is not a difficult peak to climb. The rocky slopes are challenging enough to give a real sense of fulfilment, yet the climb is so short it offers a perfect afternoon out for families and casual walkers. No wonder this is Wicklow's most popular peak, and climbed by thousands of people annually.

Given the mountain's popularity, I make no apologies for describing two routes to the summit. The first is a straightforward out-and-back trip that can be completed in little over an hour. The alternative circuit is longer, less frequented and more satisfying, and could be described as the connoisseur's route to the top. Paths are followed throughout both routes, and it is not unusual to see children as young as three years old attempting the mountain. Be warned, however, that the final ascent necessitates some hands-on scrambling over loose stones. If you are contemplating bringing young children here, it would be wise to complete the route unaccompanied first to assess the level of difficulty for yourself.

Out-and-Back from the South

Start & Finish: The short route starts and finishes a car park at the southern base of Great Sugar Loaf (grid reference: O235119). Access the area via the N11 Dublin–Wicklow road. Turn off the N11 at junction 9, which is signed for Glenview. On the western side of the N11, turn left up Red Lane. The steep, narrow road climbs to the top of the shoulder beside Great Sugar Loaf. Park on the right in a car park marked by a stone entrance arch.

The Walk

From the car park, walk around the metal gate and begin to follow a wide earthen trail towards the mountain. Climb gradually to a rock-studded area just beneath the main slopes. The path then forges uphill, over the rocks, to reach a flat area part way up the mountain's western flank.

Continue to a junction of paths, then turn right. You are now on the final ascent to the summit, and the slope is very steep. You will need to use your hands as you scramble over the rocks, and care is needed to avoid slipping on loose stones underfoot. There are several possible ascent routes over line about 5m wide. Choose between an eroded gully or the

The path from the south heads directly towards the volcano-like cone of Great Sugar Loaf.

slopes nearby; if a particular rock step is too high for you, you will generally find an easier route by stepping to one side.

The slope only relents as you arrive at the summit itself. There is no cairn to mark the high point, but the compact top provides enough natural drama that it does not matter. Rocky outcrops underfoot combine with fantastic 360° views over Dublin city, the central Wicklow Mountains and a long stretch of coastline. On a clear day you may even be lucky enough to see the peaks of Snowdonia across the Irish Sea.

Descend by reversing your outward route, taking care not to dislodge rocks onto walkers approaching from below.

Circuit from the East

Start & Finish: This circuit starts and finishes in front of Kilmacanoge GAA pitch (grid reference: O244141). From Dublin, turn off the N11 Dublin–Wicklow road at junction 8, signed to Roundwood and Glendalough. Cross to the western side of the N11, then, just before a roundabout, turn left onto Quill Road. Just 30m later, turn right up a narrow lane signed to Fitzsimmons Park GAA Grounds. Continue almost to the end of the lane, then park in a lay-by outside the GAA gates, where there is space for at least eight vehicles.

The Walk

From the parking area, join a footpath that runs along the right-hand side of the GAA grounds. This brings you to open scrubland beneath Great

Sugar Loaf. Keep right at the first fork, then take the third turn on the left, opposite a mound of boulders. Follow this trail uphill, climbing initially through gorse and scrub, then up a steep, grassy slope.

This brings you to a heather-clad col on the northern shoulder of the mountain. Turn left here, then left again to join a wide trail that runs along the ridge. There are now fine views east over the Wicklow Mountains, with Djouce particularly prominent on the skyline.

Keep left at the next junction and climb gradually around the eastern side of a hummock. Veer right at the next fork and follow a rocky path up to a flat area just west of the summit. Here you join the main path described above; turn left and scramble up the steep rock slopes to the summit.

After appreciating the summit views, return to the flat area and turn left to resume the circuit. Descend south along a rocky path until the angle of descent eases, then continue ahead for another 100m to reach a point just above a wide patch of short grass. Look carefully here to locate a faint grassy footpath that turns left off the main trail.

Follow this footpath east, with the trail consolidating underfoot as you descend. You are now heading towards the wooded valley of the Glen of the Downs. Around 400m above a farm building, turn left onto a clearer earthen path that swings left above a quarry.

At the base of the slope, keep right in front of a thicket of gorse, then turn left and right at the following two junctions. You are now back on a clear footpath that passes around the eastern base of the mountain. Descend to a copse of deciduous woodland, keeping right at a fork shortly after you enter the trees. It is not long now before the path arrives at the end of a tarmac road. Follow the road ahead, and you will find yourself back at the GAA grounds just a few hundred metres later.

The path on the northern shoulder of Great Sugar Loaf.

Mullaghcleevaun

A short but rewarding route up the second highest summit in Wicklow, with fine views over the lough on its northern side.

Grade:	4
Time:	3–4 hours
Distance:	8.5km (5½ miles)
Ascent:	570m (1,870ft)
Map:	OSi 1:50,000 sheet 56, EastWest Mapping 1:30,000 *Wicklow Mountains West*, or Harvey Superwalker 1:30,000 *Wicklow Mountains*.

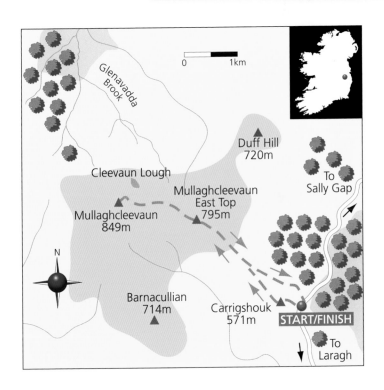

Start & Finish: The route starts and finishes at the end of a track just northeast of Carrigshouk (grid reference: O103053). There is parking space for around four vehicles at the end of the track, and several other lay-bys nearby if you need more room.

This is the easiest and most direct route to the top of Mullaghcleevaun, the second highest peak in the Wicklow Mountains at 849m. It is an out-and-back trip, and includes a visit to the summits of Carrigshouk (571m) and Mullaghcleevaun East (795m). In terms of scenery, the final 2km before the summit are the best. Here you pass along the edge of the steep corrie that cuts into the mountain's northern slopes. This corrie has even given the mountain its name: the Irish *Mullach Cliabháin* translates as 'Summit of the Basket'. The basin is filled by Cleevaun Lough, which holds the accolade of being the highest natural lake in Wicklow.

In clear conditions the views from the summit of Mullaghcleevaun extend as far as Wales, and the route presents few navigational difficulties. In poor visibility you should exercise caution near the corrie rim, and will probably need to take a compass bearing to ensure the correct line of descent. A faint path is visible in places, but elsewhere you cross untracked ground and must rely on your own route-finding skills.

The Walk

The sharp hummock of Carrigshouk is an obvious landmark from the Military Road, and features short but steep slabs on its eastern side. In good visibility the rocks can all be clearly seen from below, and it makes an interesting start to the walk to pick a route up through the outcrops to the top.

From the end of the track, walk a few metres south along the road. Leave the tarmac at the hill's northeastern base and begin to pick your way up between the rocks. One good option follows a faint path through a small gully on the hill's northeastern corner, though less steep ground can be found on the northern slopes.

From the small summit cairn there are already good views over eastern Wicklow, while to the northwest the rounded peaty ridge leading to Mullaghcleevaun East is clearly visible. Descend northwest over heather-clad slopes to reach the col beneath this mountain, then begin the gradual ascent to the top. The ground is rough at first but becomes easier as you gain height, and you should pick up a faint path as you progress.

The summit of Mullaghcleevaun East is marked by a small cairn and several interesting boulder formations. Mullaghcleevaun itself can now be seen to the west. Before you embark on the next leg of the journey, however, take a moment to study the terrain in the col beneath you. Several swathes of exposed peat spread across the saddle, and the easiest passage is to avoid these as much as possible. The best advice is to keep to the northern side of the col, where you should find an easy route that offers little resistance.

From the col, begin to climb the grassy slope ahead. Keep to the right and climb around the rim of the corrie to enjoy the best views across the lough below. This is a great piece of walking and it is hard to tear yourself away from the drama of the corrie, but to reach the official summit you must head southeast for a short distance, where you will find the mountain's trig point. Circle the edge of the small plateau to appreciate fully the fantastic views. Landmarks include Lugnaquilla to the south, and Pollaphuca Reservoir – the largest reservoir in Ireland – to the west.

The return route is essentially a reversal of your outward journey. As you descend from Mullaghcleevaun East, begin by heading towards Lough Dan to pick up the path down the shoulder. Unless you want to revisit Carrigshouk, you can vary your route by following a narrow path that drops off the northern side of the col beneath this hill. The trail descends gradually around the northern base of Carrigshouk. It joins a rutted track for a short distance, then drops left to join a better gravel track. Turn right and follow the track back to the road, where your vehicle should be waiting.

A trig point marks the 849m summit of Mullaghcleevaun.

Luggala and Knocknacloghoge

A spectacular route over neighbouring summits, above the two most iconic lakes in the Wicklow Mountains.

Grade:	4
Time:	4½–5½ hours
Distance:	12km (7½ miles)
Ascent:	780m (2,560ft)
Map:	OSi 1:50,000 sheet 56, EastWest Mapping 1:30,000 *Wicklow Mountains West* or *Wicklow East*, or Harvey Superwalker 1:30,000 *Wicklow Mountains*.

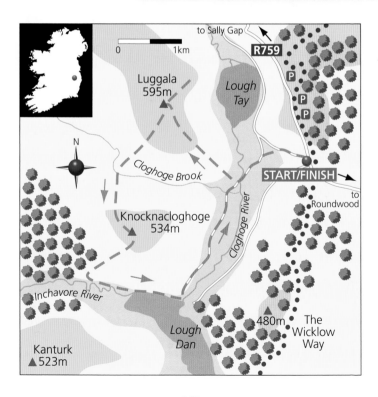

The cliffs of Luggala rise above the Cloghoge River.

Start & Finish: The route starts and finishes at the gateway known as the 'Pier Gates', located along the R759 above Lough Tay (grid reference: O173065). The gates themselves are made of black metal and set in a stone wall. Park beside a track entrance opposite the gates, or in one of several other lay-bys nearby.

Exploring two mountain summits between Lough Tay and Lough Dan, this is surely one of the most scenic walks in the Wicklow Mountains. The peaks themselves are wild and rugged, yet they are connected at their base by a strikingly beautiful valley that contains the most photographed lakes in the region. The interplay between towering cliffs and serene lakeshore, between lofty summits and fertile valley, is what makes the route so special.

The glen itself was moulded by the glaciers of the last ice age, and Lough Tay and Lough Dan are classic examples of ribbon lakes – where a series of lakes has formed at the bottom of a U-shaped valley after the ice has melted away.

Though the circuit involves no great navigational difficulties, the middle section of the route crosses rough terrain with no path, and the presence of precipitous drops means you should avoid the route in poor visibility. The crossing of the Cloghoge Brook is also awkward after heavy rain.

The Walk

Pass through the pedestrian entrance beside the Pier Gates and head downhill along the road. Either follow the road all the way to the valley floor, or look out for a wooden pole in a section of fence on the left. This marks the start of a steep footpath that will shortcut the dog-leg in the road.

As you near the valley floor, cross a stone stile beside a gate, then continue straight ahead at the next junction. The road dwindles to a gravel track and arrives at a bridge across the Cloghoge River. Cross the bridge, then quickly turn right and climb a large wooden stile.

Pass through a metal gate, then continue straight up a grassy path that climbs the slope in front of you. The path climbs steadily up Luggala's southwestern shoulder, with the grassy terrain turning to peat as you gain height. Near the top you are treated to a bird's-eye perspective down the mountain's eastern cliffs to Lough Tay.

Follow the path all the way to the summit, which is something of an anticlimax, without even a cairn to mark the high point. For more fine views over Lough Tay, consider a detour 500m northeast, following a peaty path that descends along the top of the Luggala cliffs. Though this detour necessitates a height loss – and subsequent re-ascent – of 100 vertical metres, it is well worth it for the view across the lake from the top of a cliff-fringed promontory.

Back at the summit, the circuit continues by descending southwest. The wetter the conditions, the further west you should go here, to ease your crossing of the Cloghoge Brook. Thick heather makes progress rather awkward, and once you have crossed the river, the initial part of the climb south up Knocknacloghoge also crosses rough ground covered by heather and tussock grass.

The summit of Knocknacloghoge is strewn with granite outcrops and marked by a small cairn. It also provides great views along the length of Lough Dan to the south. Now join a path that descends south past a couple of outcrops. When the trail veers southeast, turn southwest across open ground instead. The slopes here are covered with bracken, and will either provide a straightforward or awkward passage depending on the time of the year.

As you descend, aim for the forestry plantation on the northern bank of the Inchavore River. This avoids the steep crags that line the southern base of the mountain. Pick your way between the boulders to reach the river, then turn left and follow the river upstream. You will have to negotiate several marshy patches before you reach the beautiful spit of white sand that lies at the northwestern tip of Lough Dan.

Now follow a well-trodden path along the northern shore of the lough. The path is surrounded by thick gorse and can be rather overgrown in places. It exits near a deserted house at the northeastern corner of the lake. It is well worth turning right beside the house and following a smaller path for 300m to reach a lovely little beach on the lakeshore. This is an idyllic spot, frequented by swimmers and families during the summer.

When you are ready, return to the deserted house and turn right onto a grassy track. This leads up the valley past a series of fields. Pass through a couple of gates and cross a bridge to arrive at a second bridge, which you should recognise from your outward journey. Simply retrace your initial steps – unfortunately uphill this time – to return to your starting point on the road above.

ROUTE 60:
Djouce and War Hill

This circuit combines one of Wicklow's most popular summits with a trip through a wild and lonely valley.

Grade:	4
Time:	4½–5½ hours
Distance:	14km (9 miles)
Ascent:	660m (2,170ft)
Map:	OSi 1:50,000 sheet 56, EastWest Mapping 1:30,000 *The Dublin and North Wicklow Mountains* or *Wicklow East*, or Harvey Superwalker 1:30,000 *Wicklow Mountains*.

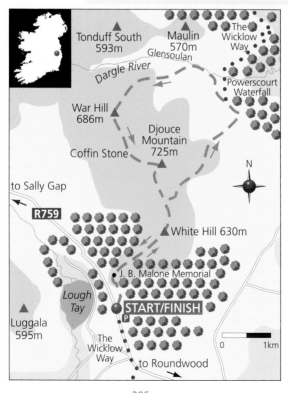

Djouce's summit trig point sits atop a rock outcrop.

Start & Finish: The route starts and finishes at a parking area above Lough Tay along the R759 (grid reference: O169075). The car park is marked by a map board for the Wicklow Way, and there is space for at least twelve vehicles. If you need more room there are several other lay-bys nearby along the road.

The focal point of this route is the summit of the popular 725m-high Djouce. This peak could be visited in a short out-and-back trip in its own right, but the addition of a circuit around the northwestern side of the mountain allows a visit to lonely Glensoulan, the summit of War Hill, and the landmark of the Coffin Stone. There are wide-ranging views over the Wicklow mountains and coastline, the early panorama across Lough Tay is quite rightly one of the most celebrated sights in the region.

The route follows the Wicklow Way for around half its distance, benefiting from the signposts, paths and boardwalk of that trail. There is also an informal path to ease your progress between the summit of War Hill and Djouce. However, the section from Glensoulan to the top of War Hill crosses wild and rough terrain that can be thick with heather, and you will need to rely on your own route-finding skills here.

The Walk

The first 4km of the route follows the Wicklow Way, and is signed by frequent waymarking posts. From the parking area, begin by heading past the map board and joining a vehicle track. Just 50m along the track, turn left onto an earthen path that weaves through a patch of clear-felled forestry. This brings you to the start of a length of boardwalk, which climbs onto the southwestern shoulder of White Hill. Before long you reach a large boulder with an adjacent plaque commemorating J. B. Malone, pioneer of the Wicklow Way. It is a fantastic viewpoint, and the sight of Lough Tay nestling beneath the cliffs of Luggala is one of the region's most impressive scenes.

Continue to follow the boardwalk over the hump of White Hill. The summits of Djouce and War Hill are now visible ahead. Descend across a stile in the col between White Hill and Djouce, then climb again, still following the walkway as it makes a steady ascent along the shoulder towards Djouce. Soon you reach a junction, where an informal path continues ahead and the boardwalk of the Wicklow Way turns sharply right. Turn right here – you will return along the other path at the end of the circuit.

The boardwalk soon comes to an end, and you contour across to the mountain's northeastern shoulder. Turn right here and descend along a broad path to reach a stone wall. Cross the wall, still following the signs for the Wicklow Way, and descend to a second stile. This is where you leave must leave the waymarked trail and begin to strike out across open country.

The Wicklow Way turns right immediately after the stile, but you should continue straight ahead, following a faint, grassy path towards the foundations of several old stone buildings below. Cross a stream with the help of a makeshift bridge then veer right, past the ruins, and descend around the northern base of Djouce. Join the bank of the nascent Dargle River and turn left to head upstream. You are now in the heart of Glensoulan, and the landscape feels pleasantly wild after the well-trodden trail of the Wicklow Way.

The untamed nature of the valley means there is no path to guide you, and progress is sometimes awkward between here and the summit of War Hill. Follow the Dargle upstream and cross the tributary that drains the valley between War Hill and Djouce. Shortly beyond this, leave the river and begin to climb the northeastern shoulder of War Hill. The heather is very thick in places, and will continue for most of the way to the top. The rounded summit itself is marked by a tiny cairn and far-reaching views, with the mast to the northwest indicating the top of Kippure.

Turn southeast at the summit and descend gradually along a faint path to reach the col below. Negotiate a few peat hags, then climb to the

Is it a megalithic portal tomb? The Coffin Stone, between War Hill and Djouce.

huge boulders that make up the Coffin Stone. This is either a suggestively placed glacial erratic or, as some commentators believe, the remains of a megalithic portal tomb, its massive capstone now partially collapsed and the remains of a courtyard visible at the front.

Continue to climb southeast from the stone, following a path to the trig point at the top of Djouce, which is set rather jauntily atop a rock outcrop. The views extend far and wide in every direction, and it is worth savouring the moment.

When you are ready, descend by following a wide trail southwest along the summit plateau. After 300m, veer left and along a steep path that brings you to the junction with the boardwalk you passed on your outward journey. Continue straight ahead onto the planks, and retrace you initial steps along the Wicklow Way to the finish.

Tonelagee

This compact route climbs around a dramatic corrie to reach the third-highest summit in Wicklow.

Grade:	4
Time:	3–4 hours
Distance:	8km (5 miles)
Ascent:	490m (1,610ft)
Map:	OSi 1:50,000 sheet 56, EastWest Mapping 1:30,000 *Wicklow Mountains West*, or Harvey Superwalker 1:30,000 *Wicklow Mountains*.

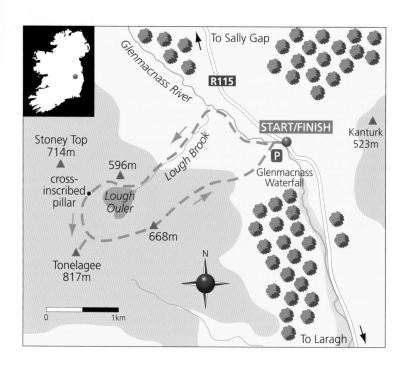

Passing Lough Ouler, with Tonelagee behind.

Start & Finish: The route starts and finishes at a large car park above Glenmacnass Waterfall (grid reference: O113030). The car park is situated beside the R115 Military Road, around 7km northwest of Laragh and 10km south of the Sally Gap.

Tonelagee, the third highest peak in Dublin and Wicklow, is a mountain with a split personality. From most angles its slopes are uniform and not particularly interesting. But approach the summit from the northeast, and you will discover a deep corrie that cuts into its flanks and provides an entirely different experience. At the base of the corrie lies heart-shaped Lough Ouler, a beautiful lake whose wild location makes it one of the most dramatic upland loughs in the region.

Tonelagee translates from the Irish as 'Backside to the Wind', which makes sense when you consider that Ireland's prevailing winds come from the southwest. Both the corrie and lake are classic features of a post-glacial landscape. Indeed the entire valley, including the magnificent 80m-high Glenmacnass Waterfall, owes its form to the scouring movement of past ice sheets.

The route is fairly straightforward from a navigational point of view. It follows informal paths for roughly half the distance, and crosses open mountainside for the rest. Note that the corrie rim is dangerous in poor visibility, and you may not be able to ford the Glenmacnass River after heavy rain (as there are no alternative crossing places, you will have to choose a different objective if this is the case).

The Walk

From the car park, walk upstream along the bank of the Glenmacnass River for roughly 80m. Here you will find a jumble of river boulders fortuitously arranged in such a way that they provide perfect natural stepping stones. Cross the river here, then turn right along the opposite bank.

Continue to follow the river for another kilometre until you reach the confluence with the outlet stream that flows down from Lough Ouler. Cross this side-stream, then turn left and begin to follow its northern bank southwest. There is a narrow path here to ease your progress through the heather.

After almost 2km you mount a rise and see the lake ahead, backed by steep corrie walls. Continue to the lakeshore, which makes a perfect spot for a break. When you are ready, follow a narrow path along the northern shore, then climb to the shallow col just west of point 596m. From here, follow a path that makes a curving ascent around the northeastern rim of the corrie, climbing steadily all the time.

Shortly before the top you will pass a small standing stone. Made of an upright slab of mica schist, the stone has a roughly carved Latin cross incised on each face. Despite its markings, archaeologists have not associated the pillar with any particular ritual, and believe it is simply an ancient boundary marker. Continue to climb around the corrie rim, then veer southwest to reach the trig pillar that marks the top of Tonelagee.

The summit views are fantastic. Amongst numerous surrounding peaks the mountains to the west stand out, where the summit reservoir of Turlough Hill is backed by the mighty bulk of Lugnaquilla. To the north, the rounded, peaty saddle of the Barnacullian ridge stretches away towards Mullaghcleevaun, providing another, longer access route to Tonelagee.

For the descent, begin by heading southeast from the trig pillar. A faint path shows the way. Now sweep east along the ridge, keeping close to the rim of the corrie for more fantastic views over the heart-shaped lough below. Descend across a shallow col and climb slightly to point 668m, still following a visible path.

Now head northwest along a broad ridge. The natural tendency here is to veer further south than necessary, so take care to keep on the correct line. The path dissipates somewhat underfoot, but continue ahead through the grass and heather, then drop down to meet the Glenmacnass River. Cross the river via the same stepping stones you used on your outward journey, then complete the final 80m downstream to the car park.

ROUTE 62:
Scarr and Kanturk

This memorable route traverses a pair of mid-height peaks, with fine views over Lough Dan and the central Wicklow Mountains.

Grade:	4
Time:	4½–5½ hours
Distance:	14km (8½ miles)
Ascent:	540m (1,770ft)
Map:	OSi 1:50,000 sheet 56, EastWest Mapping 1:30,000 *Wicklow Mountains West*, or Harvey Superwalker 1:30,000 *Wicklow Mountains.*

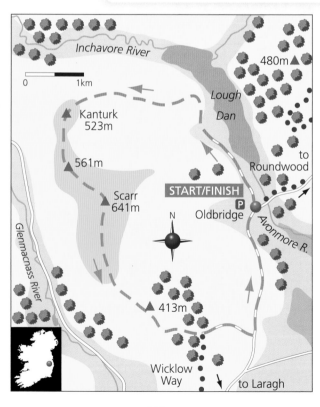

Start & Finish: The circuit starts and finishes at a lay-by in Oldbridge (grid reference: O158019). Oldbridge can be reached from Laragh or Roundwood. From Roundwood, turn west, following signs to Lough Dan. In the hamlet of Oldbridge, turn right, still following the Lough Dan signs. Park 250m later in a gravel lay-by on the left, located just before a junction with a minor road. There is enough space here for around ten vehicles.

A cursory glance at the map would not engender much excitement about climbing 523m Kanturk or 641m Scarr. But looks can be deceiving, and this is one route that most walkers find more enjoyable than they had thought possible. The route begins with a scenic treat, traversing high above the shore of beautiful Lough Dan. The summits themselves boast a surprising amount of character too, with Kanturk distinguished by a maze of rock outcrops and Scarr by its narrow summit ridge. And the massif's location in the heart of the Wicklow Mountains provides the icing on the cake, ensuring incredible views throughout.

The route follows well-defined paths across all the high ground, making navigation a relatively simple affair. There are sections of road walking at the start and finish of the circuit, with a total of almost 4km along the tarmac. These lanes see little traffic, however, and the effort is worthwhile for the route it allows.

The Walk

From the parking lay-by, begin by heading northwest along the road. Climb steadily along the tarmac, passing first through mixed forest, then through open countryside with fine views over Lough Dan, the largest natural lake in Wicklow. After 1.5km the road crosses a bridge and turns

Descending along the path on the southern shoulder of Scarr.

sharply left. Around 60m beyond the bridge, turn right onto a footpath marked by a wooden gate and a walking signpost.

Follow the path through a fenced copse of woodland, then out onto a lovely, scenic trail high above the lake. The path ends at a track after 1km; cross the track and climb a set of wooden steps on the opposite side. Cross a stile beside a large boulder, then follow a well-defined, grassy trail path that leads easily along the shoulder ahead. There are fine views north from here to the steep cliffs that bind the lower slopes of Knocknacloghoge.

As you near the top of the shoulder, the first landmark you reach is a large oval boulder that is a glacial erratic. From here the path veers south and begins to weave through a maze of hummocks and granite outcrops. Though the mountain has no defined high point, this labyrinth of features make it one of Wicklow's more memorable summits.

As you exit the maze, you are met by clear views ahead to Scarr. The path dips across a shallow hollow, past the occasional boggy patch, then makes a gradual ascent to point 561m. To the south, massive Tonelagee now dominates the scene across the Glenmacnass Valley.

Continue southeast across the col, then begin the final ascent to Scarr. Along the way you will pass a small standing stone, and also enjoy a bird's-eye view over Glenmacnass Waterfall. A final steep climb brings you to the top of the mountain. The summit ridge is enjoyably narrow, and boasts a small cairn – the first of the route – and fabulous 360° views that include many of southern Wicklow's highest peaks.

Cross straight over the summit ridge and descend south along a broad shoulder, heading towards the right-hand corner of a small forestry plantation. A clear path ensures easy passage underfoot. You reach the forest at a corner, with a rusty gate straight ahead. Turn left here and follow a rough vehicle track along the edge of the trees. Within a few hundred metres, turn right at the forest's northeastern corner and descend along the track, still keeping the plantation to your right.

At the bottom of the forest you come to a junction of tracks. Keep straight ahead here, climbing across a stile beside a metal gate. You are now on the route of the Wicklow Way, and can follow the waymarks all the way back to Oldbridge. Essentially you descend along the track to reach a road, then turn left. Follow the road over several undulations to the junction at Oldbridge, where you should turn left. Your vehicle should now be 300m away on the left.

Camaderry Circuit

A trip along Glendalough's Upper Lake leads to fine views and an enjoyable mountaintop return.

Grade:	4
Time:	4½–5½ hours
Distance:	13km (8 miles)
Ascent:	630m (2,070ft)
Map:	OSi 1:50,000 sheet 56, EastWest Mapping 1:30,000 *Lugnaquilla & Glendalough*, or Harvey Superwalker 1:30,000 *Wicklow Mountains*.

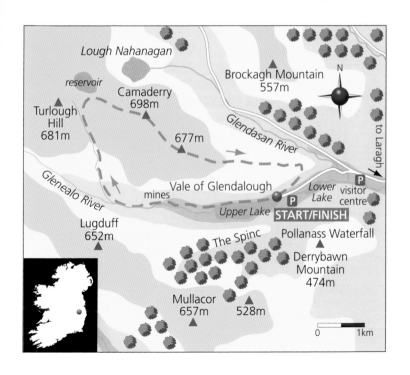

The 698m summit of Camaderry.

Start & Finish: The route starts and finishes in Glendalough, at the large car park beside Upper Lake at the end of the R757 road (grid reference: T111964). There is a €4 charge to enter the car park; have the exact change ready to pass through the automatic barrier.

This enjoyable circuit is a tale of two halves. The outward part of the route follows the popular miner's track along Glendalough's Upper Lake. There is no denying the beauty of this valley, but depending on the time of the year, you may be appreciating the scenery in the company of throngs of tourists.

Once you pass the old mine workings at the western end of the lake, and especially once you are past the Glenealo footbridge of the Spinc Loop, you will find the character of the route changes dramatically. There are few signs of passing feet and you are suddenly alone amidst wild mountain terrain. The untamed atmosphere is enhanced by the wildlife, and this is a particularly good route for spotting deer and feral goats. As you make your way along Camaderry's summit ridge you rejoin a well-defined path but the mountainous feeling continues, with fine 360° views encompassing most of Wicklow's highest peaks.

The route does not involve any notable natural hazards or navigational difficulties, but a clear day will be appreciated to make the most of the views.

The Walk

From the upper car park, begin by heading along the northern bank of Upper Lake. You have a choice of routes: take either the miner's road, a flat forest track that contours around 20m above the lake, or the footpath along the lakeshore. The shoreline path climbs to join the miner's road near the western end of the lough, and you continue past the beach and marsh at the end of the lake.

The track now passes the remnants of several former mine buildings, as well as spoil heaps and some rusted machinery. These are all legacies of nineteenth-century mining activities. The path is broken underfoot here – when the Glenealo River floods it often inundates this area, and sometimes destroys the trail.

The trail soon consolidates again, and climbs the valley headwall in a series of well-made switchbacks. The chutes and falls of the Glenealo are a constant companion during the ascent, and the section ends at a wooden footbridge across the river.

Avoid the temptation to cross the bridge; you must now strike out on your own across open mountain terrain. Continue ahead along the northern bank of the river, then follow a tributary stream that arcs northwest. Climb along this watercouse, with an intermittent, informal path visible through the grass and heather to reassure you.

Before long the distinctive, flat-topped form of Turlough Hill Reservoir comes into sight ahead. Climb steadily across rough ground to the right of the stream, negotiating several wet patches underfoot. At the top of the slope you reach the tall wire fence that encloses the reservoir. This is part of the only pumped-storage hydroelectricity plant in Ireland, which works by connecting the artificial summit reservoir with the natural corrie lake of Lough Nahanagan some 250m below.

Turn right around the perimeter of the reservoir and follow a well-worn path to the southeastern corner of the fence. The path branches off here and descends to the col beneath Camaderry, forging a fairly direct line through the peat hags that litter the saddle. An easy climb then brings you to the summit of Camaderry (698m), which has no real cairn except a couple of casual stones balanced atop a boulder. There are good views across Tonelagee and Mullaghcleevaun to the north, while the brooding bulk of Lugnaquilla can be seen to the southwest.

Descend southeast from the summit along the obvious path, climbing only slightly to pass over point 677m. Now descend a steep step, hopping across several more wet patches. The angle eases as you progress, and the peat eventually gives way to a grassy trail though an expanse of bracken.

Follow the path down into the trees, where you join the end of a forest track. Turn left and follow the track through several switchbacks until a waymarking post indicates you have joined a national park trail marked by silver arrows. Turn right here and follow the marked trail along the track. You contour across the hillside for a while before descending again and rejoining the miner's road near a stone cottage. Turn left onto the miner's road and walk the final 300m back to the car park.

The Spinc Loop

An airy, clifftop path is the highlight of this wonderfully scenic circumnavigation of Glendalough's Upper Lake.

Grade:	3
Time:	3½–4 hours
Distance:	11.5km (7 miles)
Ascent:	400m (1,310ft)
Map:	OSi 1:50,000 sheet 56, EastWest Mapping 1:30,000 *Lugnaquilla & Glendalough*, or Harvey Superwalker 1:30,000 *Wicklow Mountains*.

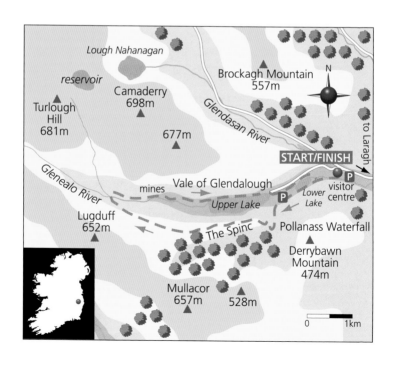

Lough Nahanagan

reservoir

Camaderry
698m

Brockagh Mountain
557m

N

Turlough
Hill
681m

Glendasan River

677m

START/FINISH

to Laragh

Glenealo River

mines

Vale of Glendalough

visitor centre

Lower
Lake

Upper Lake

Lugduff
652m

The Spinc

Pollanass Waterfall

Derrybawn
Mountain
474m

Mullacor
657m

528m

0   1km

Surveying the Glendalough Valley from the lofty vantage point of The Spinc.

Start & Finish: The route starts and finishes at the car park for the Glendalough Visitor Centre (grid reference: T126968). This is located along the R757 road, roughly 3km west of Laragh.

Of the nine waymarked walking trails in the Glendalough Valley, this route is the most popular. It climbs to the top of a long cliff on the southern side of the Upper Lake, where the exposure and the views are enough to take your breath away. Such lofty vantage points are normally the preserve of experienced hillwalkers, but this route is fully signed and follows maintained paths throughout, making it suitable for fit leisure walkers too.

The route then descends to the upper Glenealo Valley and passes the remains of a nineteenth-century mining settlement. Add a visit to Glendalough's monastic city at the beginning of the walk, and you have not just an immensely scenic route, but a historically interesting one too.

Finally, a note of warning: though the paths and signposts make this route accessible to a wide range of people, the route crosses open mountain terrain and all the normal rules of mountain walking apply. The path also passes along the top of precipitous cliffs, and the utmost care is needed near the edge.

The Walk

The walk starts beside a footbridge at the southwestern corner of the car park. Here you will find a walk information board and the first of numerous waymarking posts. The Spinc Loop is signed throughout by the white arrows.

Begin by crossing the footbridge, then turn right along the wide path known as the Green Road. After 200m you come to a footbridge on the right, which provides access to the monastic city founded by St Kevin in the sixth century. The site includes a 30m-high round tower and several monastic dwellings, and is well worth a quick detour if you have not visited it before.

When you are ready, return to the Green Road and follow it for over a kilometre, passing mature oak woodland beside the Lower Lake. You now arrive at the park information office, which is housed in a small white cottage at the southeastern corner of Upper Lake. Around 20m beyond the office, turn left up a path signed for Pollanass Waterfall.

Climb a series of steps beside the waterfall, then turn left onto a forest track. Turn right at the next junction then, 100m later, turn right again onto a narrow footpath. Climb steeply up a long flight of steps made from old railway sleepers, which forges a way uphill through a tunnel of trees.

The ground flattens out as you exit the trees, and just a few metres later you receive your first, magnificent view over Glendalough Upper Lake. The spectacular scenery will stay with you for the next kilometre as you traverse along the top of the cliffs some 200m above the water.

Most of the path along the cliffs is constructed from wooden sleepers, so it is a simple matter to follow the route forward. At the western end of the lake the sleepers split at a junction. Keep right here, and climb to the highest point of the route at just over 500m. The trail now begins to descend, dropping gently down to a footbridge over the Glenealo River.

Cross the bridge and turn right, enjoying another fine view along the Glendalough Valley ahead. A series of well-made switchbacks carries you down the valley headwall, and deposits you at the former mining settlement. This area is littered with old mine paraphernalia – spoil heaps, rusted machinery and tumbledown buildings – and the path is sometimes broken underfoot as it weaves its way through the ruins.

Continue past a marsh and wide sandy beach to reach the western end of Upper Lake. The wide gravel track known as the miner's road now contours ahead, keeping around 20m above the lake. Alternatively, if you want to walk closer to the water's edge, watch out for a small footpath that descends to the lakeshore after roughly 300m.

The shoreline path and the miner's road both deposit you at the car park at the eastern end of Upper Lake. Keep to the left side of the car park and join the end of a wooden boardwalk. This carries you easily past Lower Lake, and brings you to a junction with the Green Road just before the monastic city. Turn left here and complete the final 400m back to the start.

ROUTE 65:
Lugnaquilla

This classic route up Leinster's highest peak includes a visit to beautiful Art's Lough and dramatic Fraughan Rock Glen.

Grade:	4
Time:	5–6 hours
Distance:	13km (8 miles)
Ascent:	800m (2,620ft)
Map:	OSi 1:50,000 sheet 56, EastWest Mapping 1:30,000 *Lugnaquilla & Glendalough*, or Harvey Superwalker 1:30,000 *Wicklow Mountains*.

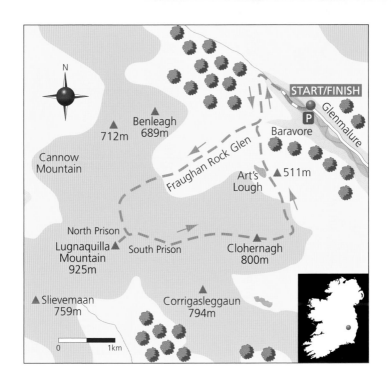

Start & Finish: The circuit starts and finishes at a large car park at Baravore, at the head of Glenmalure (grid reference: T066942). Glenmalure is generally reached via the Military Road from Laragh.

At 925m high, Lugnaquilla is Ireland's thirteenth highest mountain. It is the highest summit in the province of Leinster, and the highest point in the country outside County Kerry. On a clear day from the summit, views encompass much of Wicklow, South Leinster and even Wales.

The route begins at the head of Glenmalure, and is my favourite way to approach the mountain. The terrain and the scenery are dramatic and varied, and the circuit is conveniently compact. The route starts and finishes in the cliff-fringed valley of Fraughan Rock Glen, though the jewel in the crown is the high, secluded lake of Art's Lough, a hidden gem set amidst a wild landscape that is surely one of Wicklow's most beautiful sights.

Finally, a word of warning: Lugnaquilla is notorious for its bad weather, and is covered by cloud five days out of seven. The summit plateau is bordered by steep cliffs that surround the twin corries of the North Prison and South Prison, and navigation can also be tricky on the descent from Cloghernagh back to Fraughan Rock Glen. The paths here are most accurately displayed on the EastWest Mapping sheet, but enough hazards remain that the route is best avoided in poor visibility.

The Walk

At the northwestern corner of the car park, there is a road ford across the Avonbeg River. Turn right in front of the ford and follow a footpath upstream for 100m, then cross the river via a footbridge. On the opposite bank, turn right onto a vehicle track. Continue past the building of the Glenmalure Youth Hostel, then turn left at a track junction.

The track leads steadily uphill through the forest, then out into the more open surrounds of Fraughan Rock Glen. The scenery here is immediately impressive, with the Benleagh cliffs towering overhead on your right. You will also notice a forestry plantation on the southern side of the valley; you will descend along the western edge of these trees at the end of the circuit.

For now, follow the track to the base of a waterfall, then climb steeply up the right-hand side of the falls. Pass over the lip of the headwall into the rugged hanging valley above. Keep following the bank of the main stream to the top of another rise. Continue across a boggy hollow, then climb straight up the slope ahead. You can choose your line of ascent depending on how steep you want the climb to be – the slope is steepest to the south and tapers off to the north. Salvation awaits at the ridgeline, where the rough ground is instantly replaced by a gentle slope of close-cropped grass, which provides a perfect walking surface across the entire summit plateau.

Turn left when you reach the top of the ridge, and the prominent summit cairn will soon come into view to the south. Walk diagonally across the plateau to reach it. Lugnaquilla's trig point sits atop a massive circular plinth and offers predictably fine 360° views, with a nearby orientation plaque to help you identify the landmarks.

Your next goal is Cloghernagh. Sweep northeast around the rim of the South Prison before heading east along a broad ridge to Cloghernagh. A wide path along the top of the shoulder makes for easy progress. The 800m summit itself is distinguished by a small cairn, and expansive views to the east.

Take care now to locate the correct descent route to Art's Lough, which is hidden from view below. From Cloghernagh, follow a faint path that descends east for 200m, then veers northeast to the top of the cliffs on the northern edge of the shoulder. At the western corner of the cliffs, turn left onto another narrow path that is marked by occasional cairns of white stone.

This path traverses north along the top of the drop, then begins to descend along a grassy ramp. A short distance later, Art's Lough comes into view below. The ramp carries you almost all the way to the lake. You will now see a wire fence that runs parallel to the lake, just above its eastern shore. Follow this fence north to a corner then turn right, following a boggy path along the left side of the fence. Descend steeply beside a forestry plantation, heading back towards Fraughan Rock Glen.

Towards the bottom of the slope, veer left slightly and pass through a gate around 150m west of the forest. Cross the river, then climb the opposite bank to join the main track through the glen. Turn right here and retrace your initial steps back to the start.

View over Art's Lough, beneath the northern face of Cloghernagh.

*Surveying the Connemara landscape from the
summit of Benbrack. Twelve Bens, County Galway.*